Letters from Lee:
One Man's Story of Vietnam

LaRayne M. Topp

As told by Lee Heckman

DEDICATION

To all First Cavalry Air Mobile Reconnaissance Scouts

and to all those who didn't come home

CONTENTS

PREFACE

"I was so bitter, at least for ten years I was mad at the world. I thought I was doing the right thing going to Vietnam. No one in my family had served in the military, but I didn't have a choice. I thought I would volunteer for the draft, speed it up, get it over with. I volunteered for every training for Vietnam. I gave my country the best service I could and when I came home I was spit at and called a baby killer. It just sucked. Do you know how to spell that?"

This began my introduction to the world of Vietnam, and my feeble attempts to explain the horror that was war. To the letters of a young Lee Heckman, a farm boy from Hadar, Nebraska, who—along with other young men—were escorted by plane to United States military bases intermittently scattered across a tropical country in Southeast Asia. To the thoughts of a middle-aged man looking back at

 a time of innocence, when a fast car, some classic hit songs, a girl on his arm and a cold beer were all any young man needed to live a full life.

1

All that changed for Lee Heckman with one word: Vietnam. Before that time Lee hadn't been shot at, balancing from the door frame of an H-13 Loach as Russian-made AK-47 assault rifles fired bullets straight at him, with his name most certainly carved into the metal casings.

Until then, Lee didn't know what it was like to site an enemy down the barrel of an M-16 rifle and pull the trigger. He'd never had to write the day's flight plan for the only married man in his unit and two hours later identify his torso.

Before Lee placed his foot on base at the jungle-canopied Quan Loi in Vietnam, he'd slept a rest-filled sleep. Now, beyond a few hours a night, he hasn't slept for 40 years. Nightmares torment him when he does, as he breaks out in a cold sweat, kicking, screaming and running to escape an approaching enemy. He programs himself not to sleep and roams the dark house instead.

"Why?" I ask. "Are you back in Vietnam in your dreams? What do they say?"

"A dream is a dream," he answers.

"What one thing gives you nightmares?" I ask again.

"How many reasons did you come across?" he asks me, my hands on pages of notes, on piles of video tapes bloodied with images of war. He reaches into the pile of information and hands me a paper that tells of drowning, and mumbles something about his uncle drowning, his father's near drowning. The paper tells of the first mission Lee flew to rescue a lone, surviving crew member from a downed chopper, the soldier crouching in the elephant grass below on the banks of a river in South Vietnam. Lee covers the man's back, firing incessantly at the enemy as the rescued soldier clings to the helicopter's skids, and the chopper heads to a safe location.

"I got an award right off the bat, fishing a man out of a creek. It was a good way to start," Lee says, referring to his commendation medal for heroism.

Lee entered the Army on November 15, 1967, and was discharged on November 14, 1969. He married his sweetheart a few months later, on February 14th, 1970. When Lee came home he eliminated any military association. He let his hair grow long and he didn't talk about Vietnam. Fifteen years later he and his wife were divorced.

"Maybe if I could have talked about Vietnam...," he says, letting the sentence drift.

He carries in his soul two lives: a normal American life and the one he left behind—a normal life he can talk about and a war life he has found difficult to share.

"Nobody wants to hear about it. People don't care. Really, people don't understand," he says.

When Lee does mention his time in the service, he finds the listener is soon talking about the weather. Some veterans hook up with old buddies and converse, but Lee's buddies from basic training ended up in different locations for advanced training and eventual deployment or stateside service. They don't share the same experiences.

Because, you see, most of Lee's platoon died in Vietnam. But not all at once.

For Vietnam soldiers, the return home was not the celebrated homecoming of World War II. Those G.I.s arrived in the states together after serving together, where there was kissing and hugging and welcoming them home. Veterans of Vietnam, instead, received condemnation from numerous individuals who'd watched the war on the nightly news from the safety of their living room, where judgments on who was killed and how many were killed and how they were killed were made indiscriminately. Not understanding that war is

war, and killing on both sides takes place whether in the jungles of Vietnam, the hills of Korea, the beaches of WWII or the trenches of WWI, blanket disapproval could be thrown over all who served.

Lee hands me a photograph, with a camera angle shot from the ground up.

"I was taller in the service," he says with a smile.

He hands me a second photograph. In muted shades of Army green and brown, the photo shows twisted hunks of metal, mowed down trees and vegetation where a once powerful U.S. helicopter had writhed in the dirt just a few days before, twisting off rotors, torching its engine, spewing out the bodies of bruised and bloodied soldiers. Lee's was one of them.

"That was also me down there," he says.

Lee was a soldier in air reconnaissance in Vietnam. His job was to fly over the enemy, to attract the enemy, to get shot at by the enemy so that U.S. forces could locate the enemy.

"It isn't a bragging thing," Lee says some 40 years later. "I don't talk about it too much. Whatever I did, people had worse jobs. Our job was to observe. We were scouts. Our job was to get shot at."

What follows is the story of one man looking back, over his shoulder, at war: one young man's experiences, one young man's achievements, one seasoned man's regrets and truth. They are intermingled with thoughts from his letters—sometimes humorous, always genuine— he wrote from his Army bunk to his girlfriend back home, Barbara Toelle. His words seem at times  irreverent, but war is nasty business and Lee knows it. Always has been; always will.

"I don't want to come out in this book as a headhunter," he says. "I don't put that on my resumé. But I call a spade a spade. I did my job."

Lee Heckman was born on May 26, 1948, to Leon and Leona Heckman. He was a farm kid from Hadar, a village of about 300, nestled into the rolling hills of Northeast Nebraska. He attended a country school—Madison County District #43—where kids in grades Kindergarten through eighth grade learned spelling and arithmetic, grammar and penmanship, science and health in the same, one room. They listened to each other's classtime conversations, raising their hands to go to the bathroom located outside on the one-acre tract. He graduated from Norfolk Senior High in 1966 along with 202 others.

Lee had two sisters older than he was. "My momma never raised no idiots," he said with a grin, "but I *do* have two sisters."

Lee learned how to work growing up on the farm. When he was old enough to drive a tractor his dad rented two more farms.

"We had a dull life. We were slaves," he said.

His grandpa owned the farm, so his dad could never call the

Lee and sisters
Diane, back row, and Lois

shots or make changes. Instead, Lee's dad consoled himself by spending time in the bar.

When Lee was five years old he drove the tractor; when he was ten he was combining corn and plowing the fields. He would often plow all night. Lee and his dad did lots of farming, and eventually Lee ran all of the farm equipment. In return Lee got $100—the price of a pile of corn—for a year's work.

When Lee was a junior in high school he got a work permit to leave the school building early in the day for employment. Because Lee's dad didn't give him an allowance, anything Lee wanted—car payments, gas, entertainment—he paid for himself. While in his junior and senior years in high school he spent 60 hours a week working at a local poultry plant, cracking eggs and processing chickens during the evenings and on weekends. He earned $100 a week instead of $100 for a year's work.

Eventually, through a friend of a friend he met Barbara Toelle who grew up in an equally small town about 40 miles from Hadar.

It was to Barbara that he put pen to paper as he explored his new life at Vietnam. He wrote his girlfriend things he didn't write his mother.

Some things he hasn't even told God.

* * *

Pvt. Lee Heckman
Fort Lewis, Washington
November 16, 1967

Dear Barbara,
Well I finally got a minute to write. I'm writing real bad so it will take you longer to read it and you think it's longer than it really is. We haven't had time to sleep outside of doing our personal things.

We finally left Omaha at 7:20 and flew to Minneapolis. From there we flew to Seattle, Washington. We then took a bus and got off at Fort Lewis (Where we're at now) at about 12:30 at night. We filled out papers and stuff until 3:30 in the morning. We slept 1 ½ hours and ate and then got our heads shaved (Haircut). It costs us 90¢. We then started to learn how to stand at attention and <u>march</u>.

I'm glad I went to Universal Trade School because there are only 4 of us that graduated higher than from high school. Us 4 are the squad leaders. There are 50 in our group called a platoon. We line up in 4 rows and us 4 are the leaders of each row. It's no big deal but it's kind of nice because we don't have to do any K.P., details or fire guard. We just tell the other guys to do it and see that it gets done. Hope I keep it because when on the assigned jobs you sure get pushed around. We got the guys to wax the floor right now.

Tonight we went to the P.X. (company store) and bought $12 of supplies. We can't do anything on our own. We do only as we are told or get balled out. It's really kind of fun because someone always screws up.

Out of time,
Love, Lee
P.S. Don't write because our address will change and we won't get it.

2

Dear Barb,

It's 10:30 Saturday morning and we got a little time. I guess we usually don't do anything on Saturday or Sunday.

The weather up here is sure damp. It rains about every day and gets kind of cold.

We only got about a half an inch of hair on our heads. We get a haircut every week. Food isn't too bad but we don't get enough of it. We get up at 5:00 a.m. By 6 we are ready and marched to the mess hall. We have to choose 14 men out of our platoon to serve us. You don't get any friends when you choose the men but you at least don't have to do it yourself.

After we eat (about 10 minutes) us four leaders have to get our men back in formation. We then practice marching. I kind of like marching because it isn't any harder than walking and it keeps you warm. I feel sorry for the other men on details because like last night every two hours three men had to get up and work at the reception station.

Our barracks are very old so we have to have a fire guard on duty all night. Every hour a new man takes over. Some guys had the duty at the reception station plus fire guard duty. That didn't leave them much time for sleep. Guess I'm lucky to be a squad leader because I don't have to do any of this work.

I'm going to give a pint of blood one of these days. If we do we get the afternoon off. We only had six shots so far and they didn't even hurt. I got type O positive blood.

I hope this letter doesn't get too long that you get tired of reading it.

Our actual base combat training doesn't start until the 27ᵗʰ so it will be the last of January before we're done. Basic is 8 weeks.

Our drill sergeant says about 50% of us will go to Viet Nam. I'm not too worried because I have a little more education than most of the guys. I don't think it's really that bad anyhow. It might even be kind of fun. I guess the army is the place for me because I enjoy tough things. You can't have everything easy or it would not be any fun.

Don't write until I get you my permanent address. I'll save the rest for my next letter.
An old G.I.
Pvt. Lee Heckman

* * *

Before World War II the entire country of Vietnam was a part of French Indochina, along with Cambodia and Laos. By the end of World War II, which ended in the summer of 1945, much of the area had come under French control. The Indochina War followed in which the *Vietminh*, or Revolutionary League for the Independence of Vietnam, defended itself against France.

Communist nations recognized the Democratic Republic of Vietnam as the government of the country, while non-communist nations claimed it was the French-backed State of Vietnam. Still others claim communist expansionism was directed by the Soviets. It was difficult to ascertain which forces had the best interests of the country of Vietnam at heart.

Battles followed. A peace agreement in 1954 resulted in the division of Vietnam, with the northern half controlled by communist leaders.

The Vietnam War—also known as the Second Indochina War or the Vietnam Conflict—had its beginnings as early as 1957, when the Communist North Vietnam decided that South Vietnam looked like a country it would enjoy having under its thumb. Vietnamese Communists, intent on overthrowing the existing government, took the form of guerrillas and terrorists—known as *Viet Congsan* or Viet Cong.

The Viet Cong were supported by North Vietnam and consisted of people from both the South and the North. The official Vietnamese history of the war states that the Liberation Army of South Vietnam, or the Viet Cong, was a branch of the North Vietnamese Army, also known as the People's Army of Vietnam. Many of the Viet Cong's officers, trained in North Vietnam, secretly infiltrated South Vietnam and went to work.

The South Vietnamese Army fought back, receiving military and economic aid from the United States. In the 1950's, U.S. advisors lent their expertise as well. Then, France stepped back; the U.S. stepped in.

In 1965, the United States sent U.S. Marines to South Vietnam to protect American bases there, establishing the Marines as the first U.S. ground troops in the war. Also in 1965, the U.S. Army, Navy, Marines, Air Force and Coast Guard sent combat units with the goal of helping keep South Vietnam free from communism, joining with South Korea, Australia, New Zealand and Thailand who sent troops with the same purpose in mind. The bombing of military targets in North Vietnam began.

Communist allies Russia and Red China chose to team up with North Vietnam, supplying the Communists not with troops, but with war materials. These materials were plentiful and included medical supplies, arms, tanks, planes, helicopters, artillery, anti-aircraft missiles and other military equipment.

Toward the last decade of the war, Soviet Armed Forces joined in the melee, plus Soviet military schools and academies began training Vietnamese soldiers.

Viet Cong attacks in South Vietnam grew steadily heavier in the late 1950's and early 1960's, until the Vietnam War grew into a major conflict, with fierce battles raging throughout South Vietnam.

LaRayne M. Topp

3

Dear Barb,

Well it's Wednesday at 1730 hours. I finally got time to write. Please write if you can find time. Tell everyone Hi for me and tell them I'm fine.

I hope you've been a good girl and not getting into too much trouble. You know I have because we're restricted to the barracks and all that's there is 50 ugly guys.

Monday we had our personal interviews and applied for the jobs we wanted. We got a 50-50 chance of getting what we want. I applied for mechanics. I guess I passed all the exams except for one – infantry. I sure won't complain if they don't want me in there. I don't see how I passed the typing test but they said I did. They said not to get too many hopes up because they still can put me in the infantry. I was in the 1/4th of our platoon that passed tests and qualified for helicopter pilot.

They called us in and gave us the story. There is 36 weeks of school, 1-2 extra years of enlistment, and a sure ride to Viet Nam. Wages were real good but I didn't sign up.

We moved to our new barracks Monday. Two of us squad leaders and an arms man who takes care of the weapons got our own private room. We got radios and are trying to live it up. We cleaned all the windows inside and out, washed all the walls and swept the floor this afternoon. Kind of like your house cleaning I guess. Beds have to be made to perfection. Most of the guys are looking at the light side of things and always clowning around so things don't get too dull. We are always busy doing something so we don't have time to worry or think about home. I guess that's OK. Otherwise we would all get pretty homesick more than we are.

Some nut is always yelling attention and getting everyone excited. Then the Sarg yells attention and everyone thinks it's a false alarm and starts swearing. The Sarg sure gets mad and everyone laughs at what everyone said.

Saturday about 7:30 a new guy marched us to the P.X. He marched us across a field. There was a big pile of dirt and a bunch of guys fell down in the dark and got stomped on. Everyone laughed even though it wasn't suppose to be funny. We aren't suppose to buy candy or anything at the P.X. but we all did Saturday anyhow because a new guy took us over there. So we been smuggling goodies all week.

Have quite a few guys from Norfolk and Stanton. It's nice having guys from the same town so you can tell old stories. Everyone in our platoon is from the Dakotas or Nebraska. We are going to the P.X. tonight and then to the snack bar. I don't think we will do anything tomorrow but go to church and eat because of Thanksgiving.

Did you go home for Thanksgiving? I guess my mother went to Omaha. How does that old watch of yours run? Don't forget and say Hi to your folks too. Today we went to the dental lab for a checkup. I had to take extra x-rays and about fell to sleep in the chair.

There are three other platoons in competition with us. The top two each week get to go to the dayroom on weekends and play records, pool, etc. The last two do all the details. I doubt if we'll make the top two with all the clowns in our platoon.

We got our dog tags last week. You will die laughing when you see my ID card. I look like a bald eagle. We get a haircut every Friday. We shave and take a shower every night. All of us and our equipment must be spotless. We are wearing helmets now. We go to bed at 9:30 and get up at 5:30.

2020 hours and Thanksgiving Day
We had all we could eat for dinner. I got a big drumstick. We got to talk and take as long as we wanted. I slept about two hours this afternoon. We ate supper at 4 p.m. They stuffed us again. I think I gained about 10 lbs. Sarg said he is going to run it off us next week. He showed us how to fold all our clothes and arrange our stuff for inspections.

Sarg said most of our training will be in the classroom. We will have at least 1 hr. of exercises a day. It sounds pretty easy.

I heard on the radio Nebraska lost its football game again.

At the end of basic if all us guys take a leave together we can get a cut rate on an air force plane. It costs $97 for a trip to Omaha and back. I'm taking one $37.50 bond a month. So it might take a quite a few months to save money. Maybe I can get a new car when I get out. I wish it was about the 27ᵗʰ of Jan. so I could see you again.

Have you been checking on my mother? You should go over and cheer her up once in a while. I hope I don't repeat anything too often but I'm running out of news. Well I have to get some guys to buff and sweep the floor now.

Be good, Lee

P.S. Only 722 days left.

* * *

Lee Heckman was just a farm boy from Hadar, Nebraska. No one in his immediate family had ever been in the service, and he could have refused going to combat as a sole surviving son. But he didn't.

On November 15, 1967, he went into the Army. He was only 19 years old.

It was inevitable, he said. Your choices as a young man were to get married, have kids, go to college, or get drafted. He decided to get it over with while undergoing the least amount of pain. He took his physical and volunteered for the draft.

The military draft, also called conscription, selected people for military service determined by the nation's need for military manpower. Up until the time of the Vietnam War, the United States used a draft during the Civil War, World War I and World War II.

U.S. involvement in world affairs—plus a continuing state of tension—precipitated the draft from 1948 through 1972. This state of tension involved political conflict, military tension and economic competition, primarily between the Soviet Union and the United States, and came to be known as the Cold War. The Cold War precipitated many decisions made by legislators and the ruling president during the Vietnam War.

The country's commitment to the Vietnam War was a driving force for the draft during that time. In fact, of the 9.2 million men serving in the military between 1964 and 1975, nearly one-third served in the Vietnam theater of operations.

In 1969, the United States implemented a draft lottery in which a chance drawing of the birth dates of young men classified as 1-A took place per county in each state. This drawing paired the first birth date drawn with the number 1, ending with the men whose birth date was paired with the highest number needed to fill the draft call in each county. The men who remained were given a 1-H classification.

Men with *lucky* numbers either waited for their number to be called, volunteered for the draft or enlisted. Middle-aged men serving on the draft boards across the country found themselves pressured by mothers and fathers to exempt their sons from military service.

The Selective Service granted exemptions and deferments to college and graduate students. Of these, students who volunteered for military service and those who were drafted had a much better chance than their less-educated draftees of securing a preferential posting. This caused a sense of resentment among the poor and working class young men who couldn't afford a college education and viewed the system as unjust.

The names of married men, along with the names of married men with children, were oftentimes placed at the bottom of the list. Accordingly, it was not surprising that men rushed with their girlfriends to the altar.

Some men were exempted because of the types of jobs they held or were disqualified for physical reasons or mental deficiencies. Criminal records also gave their holders a dodge from Vietnam. Divinity students were exempt from the draft, so the number of those donning the vestments of the ministry and the rabbinate reached lofty heights during the time of the draft. Others declared exemption due to conscientious objection status.

Still others turned to what they believed could be a relatively safer alternative to the Army or the Marine Corp, the Navy or Air Force, and enlisted in the National Guard or the Army Reserves, hoping that they would avoid becoming the handful of Guard or Reserve soldiers sent to Vietnam.

Some young draftees believed that the Vietnam War was an immoral war and refused to step up when their number was called. A number of young men opposed to the draft lit a match to their draft cards and flat out refused to be inducted, going to any extreme to avoid fighting in what had become an increasingly unpopular war. As many as 100,000 draft eligible males fled the United States and moved to other countries, particularly Canada where draft evasion was not a criminal offense. A number of draft resisters were imprisoned because of their stand.

Lee Heckman originally signed up for the Seabees, a construction battalion of the U.S. Navy. The Seabees, dating back to World War II, built bases, paved miles of roadways and airstrips, and completed other construction projects. A term in the Seabees, he was told, was a two-year commitment.

As Lee was scanning the papers to join the ranks of Navy Seabees, he realized he would be signing up for a 3-year commitment. So instead, he volunteered for the draft for the U.S. Army, a two-year commitment.

As he said, "I would have been drafted within a month anyway."

LaRayne M. Topp

4

Dear Barbara,

Well I see you finally wrote me a letter. I had been gone 11 days and wrote about a dozen letters and hadn't got a word back. I gave up writing until I got your letter. If you don't want to write me please tell me. I sure miss you and any word from you makes me feel better. Some of the guys get from 2-7 letters a day. When you write please tell me everything that happens. Even if it's a bunch of nothing it's just nice hearing from you. If you aren't interested in what I'm doing please tell me and I won't go rambling on. It makes me feel good to be able to talk to the outside world and tell them what I'm all doing. You told me once that you wasn't much on writing love letters but try your best. I'm not either but I'm at least learning how to write.

Now that I got that written I'll try and write something in a better mood.

How much did it snow in Nebraska?

I hope your hair grows out by the time I see you so I won't have to laugh at them but you can just laugh at mine what's left of them.

Gosh I sure hope I can clear up my language when I get home. You can just imagine what is all said among 50 guys. The drill sergeants are always using all kinds of 4 letter words to express their views. Please express all your thoughts in your letters as you can see I do.

Our platoon is suppose to hold the record as being the best on Fort Lewis. Each cycle an award is given to the best and our Sergeant is set on getting it at all costs. You should see the way we have to clean the barracks. Beds have to be made perfect, shoes setting just so and no dust or dirt anywhere. It's hard to do with these old buildings. Us 4 squad leaders and platoon guide have got balled out the last three mornings for not getting the place clean.

He keeps threatening to take our stripes away from us. This means back to regular duty and details. Once in a while I get so tired at getting balled out that I feel like taking my stripes off and telling him to shove them. But I guess I won't. He gave us the position of acting corporal. Orders are to kick a?? all the time and see that stuff gets done. Some of these dumb heads just have to be pushed all the time. They don't realize they have to do things themselves instead of having it done for them.

Friday afternoon we marched for about 3 hours and Saturday 2 hours and Sunday 1 hour. We have our rifles now and have to stack them just so. Our rifles are M14's. Tomorrow morning we are suppose to go on a 20 mile hike. I hope not because my feet and legs are sore enough as it is.

They got some real sharp pillowcases at the P.X. with U.S. Army written on them. Tell me if you want one.

I have to get to work.

Love, Lee

* * *

Basic Training was made up of two parts: Basic Combat Training and Advanced Individual Training. Lee underwent basic training at Fort Lewis, Washington. He went on to complete Advanced Individual Training, referred to in his letters as AIT, at Fort Knox, Kentucky. On his way to basic, he took the bus from his small hometown to the big city of Omaha, and flew from Omaha to Fort Lewis, Washington, arriving there at around 4 a.m. It was a far stretch for a Nebraska farm boy.

Lee had attended the Universal Trade School at Omaha following high school graduation. While there he took mechanics classes, and found once he enlisted that furthering his education worked to his advantage. As his letters state, there were few recruits who had an education beyond high school. Those who did were selected to be squad leaders.

Basic training lasted for eight to ten weeks, and during that time individuals were taught the fundamentals of becoming a soldier, from combat techniques to the proper way to address a superior. Trainees underwent rigorous physical training as they prepared their bodies for the eventual physical strain of combat. They also developed self-discipline, brought about by a strict daily schedule and high expectations from superior officers. Marksmanship, drills, first aid and land navigation were among the fundamental military skills each trainee was expected to master.

At basic training they would work the hell out of you, Lee said, but he was a farm kid and stocky. He didn't have it as bad as some kids.

The first order of business for recruits was the head shave for men, physical examination and inoculations, and distribution of uniforms and personal gear.

A portion of Lee's letters back home described the first days of basic training: *I got three minutes to write this letter. I'm sure tired. My smallpox shot is all puffed up and the shot in my other arm is all black and blue. The fun part is we did about 75 pushups today. We're learning guerilla warfare, and bayonets, and hand to hand combat. It's kind of ruff being left handed cause all moves are just the opposite.*

Beginning the first week, recruits were taught how to march, along with body movements for standing at attention and at ease. Some recruits couldn't tell their right from their left, Lee said, so officers put a 10-pound rock in one hand of those soldiers who were confused.

"After several days of that they knew their right from their left," Lee said.

The next order of business was the upkeep of barracks, with a barrack designated for each platoon.

Punishment for not keeping an orderly barracks was swift, as Lee explained in one of his letters: *Yesterday the barracks next to us must have done something wrong. The guys had to run around the barracks, go back in, take off some clothes and run again. This kept up until all they had on was bath towels. Boy it was sure cold too.*

One guy from Lee's platoon didn't like to take showers, Lee said, so the recruits got him in the shower and all took turns with a scrub brush, Lee included. He was the first in the shower after that.

"We took care of our own," Lee explained.

Training also took place in the classroom, where recruits were taught the seven Army Core Values: loyalty, duty, respect, selfless service, honor, integrity and personal courage, spelling out the acronym for LDRSHIP (leadership). A number of examples for each skill and premise were expected to be thoroughly learned and memorized by recruits.

At the mess hall, recruits were allowed only five minutes to eat. They were never allowed to talk; only to ask for the salt and pepper. Even if they weren't through eating, the next shift was let in.

"They starved us," Lee said. "When you work as hard as we did, you're hungry."

On one of the first days Lee was at basic training he made his way to the mess hall for lunch. An officer met him at the door and asked him about the daily dozen exercises all were expected to learn. "Pvt. Heckman, what's exercise number two?"

Lee didn't know the answer. "It was only my second day there. How would I know?" Lee said.

As a result everyone in Lee's platoon was forced to drop for pushups.

"Fifty pushups was the common denominator," Lee explained.

Subsequently, with 50 trainees in his platoon, Lee said, he had 50 people on his tail.

The next day, when the officer asked recruits for examples of the dozen daily exercises, Lee knew them all.

5

Dear Barb,

How is everything in Norfolk and Beemer? We have been doing pretty good on our inspections of the barracks. Today we got 117 points out of a possible 127. The next highest platoon only got 88. They called off the inspection because we were so far ahead. We sure got mad.

Anywhere else you get shoes and break them in for your feet but not in the army. You break your feet in for your shoes.

We have been seeing lots of films. All 200 of us do exercises at once. When someone screws up we all have to do more push-ups. Tomorrow we get our eyes checked. Monday we have to run the mile, crawl 40 yards in 23 seconds and climb overhanging bars with our hands for one minute. We also have our daily dozen exercises. It sounds funny to hear all the groans and moans during exercises.

Boy the transportation rates from here to Norfolk are terrible. It costs $102.11 to fly <u>one way!</u> About going to that party in Beemer. It's up to you if you want to go to those parties. Just be a good kid and keep a good name. There isn't anything wrong with parties. Thanks for writing me. I guess I told you all about that in my last letter.

We got another haircut Monday night. I think I got more hair on my *face than on top of my head.*

They keep expressing the importance of basic training because about 90% of us are suppose to go to Viet Nam.

I'm learning how to polish shoes. Two of the guys in our platoon got dear daddy letters already. Saturday we are going to have an inspection on all our lockers and personal items.

How is that Ford running? How is work? Send that newspaper with my name in it. If you want to, send me some of your good cooking.
Tired, Lee
P.S. Be good

❖ ❖ ❖

The Army identified a series of acronyms each recruit was expected to learn. One after another, beginning with a soldier's BCT or Basic Combat Training, when a soldier received his MOS (military occupational specialty), running through his training at AIT (Advanced Individual Training) and/or LPC (Leadership Preparation Classes), a combination of letters quickly stood in for more lengthy terms.

While in training, the recruits were lined up for PT (Physical Training) or placed in FTC (a Fitness Training Company) sometimes referred to as Fat Camp. FTC involved daily, rigorous physical training and diets monitored by MFTs (Master Fitness Trainers). They also undertook CLS, a first aid training known as Combat Life Saver. Recruits were trained in evaluating and treating combat casualties and heat casualties, such as dehydration.

Fire Guard duty was coupled with CQ (Charge of Quarters). Every evening, at least two recruits from each platoon were expected to patrol their barracks area, watching for fires, cleaning the barracks and watching for recruits attempting to leave the barracks area. When their hour-long watch was through they awakened the next recruits to take over their fire guard. Similarly, Charge of Quarters shifts rotated throughout the entire company, with just two recruits from the company staying awake through an entire shift. They performed similar duties as the fire guard shift.

A soldier could receive a discharge from basic training before the completion of 180 days of training, which could be either honorable or less than honorable. This might include an EPTS, a discharge due to any condition Existing Prior To Service, or an ELS (Entry Level Separation) when a recruit demonstrated unsatisfactory performance.

6

Dear Barb,

Your last letter rather shocked me. After reading the greeting I immediately had to read the signature because I couldn't think of anyone who would write something that mushy. You must have been in a real good mood, love sick or putting on. I'm sure you meant it and I appreciate it.

Like I said don't mail that Christmas present 'cause I'll collect it in person. Don't write any letters after the 12th 'cause I won't be around to read them.

I really thought I was going to die today. We had that P.T. test. It is the same as the one we must take to graduate. It was just a check to see how bad we were. I crawled 40 yards in 32 seconds. On the mile run it was just murder. I ran it under 8.5 minutes and qualified. I got a total of 304 points out of 500. We need 300 to graduate. So with all our training I should even do better.

Boy we sure got some screwballs in our platoon. We had to fill out information forms. We got one little guy (90 lbs. 5 ft. tall). On his police record he was fined $500 for <u>attempted rape</u>. Guess he better pick on people his own size. I had to do errands and office work from 10-12 Sun. morning and from 12-2 Mon. morning. All I was suppose to do was answer phone calls. I didn't have one call. I just watched t.v. and read Playboy.

We got another shot today for the plague. Ha-ha. I got it.

Last week we got a smallpox shot and it's all swelled up. Sore arms are great on pushups.

Oh about seeing my mother do as you think. I don't know how she feels by now. She should be getting over everything.

Wasn't that a dumb post card I sent you? Couldn't think of anything to write.

If you can't think of anything to write tell me what's new in the newspapers.

Say Hi to all the girls for me.

It's about 9:30 and lights go out.

Love, Lee

✷ ✷ ✷

Basic training incorporated hand-to-hand combat and other physical challenges, plus instruction in combat maneuvers. Recruits navigated through obstacle courses at extreme heights, with an emphasis on teamwork. They rappelled down 50-foot walls with rope harnesses, trained with pugil sticks, and were sent to the gas chamber. Soldiers were subjected to CS gas, or tear gas, while wearing protective masks.

Yesterday we went to the gas chamber, Lee wrote. *We got to smell tear gas, chlorine gas, riot gas and one other. Real blast.*

They also were introduced to their weapons, and were trained in marksmanship techniques and maintenance tasks to clean, disassemble and reassemble a rifle. Later on, as they became familiar with heavier weapons, physical training became more intense. Soldiers were expected to demonstrate proficiency in the weapons in which they were trained before moving on to the next phase of training.

They took physical training twice a day and as Lee sometimes said in his letters, "They ran the hell out of you."

Recruits were pushed to such extremes that Lee could sleep standing up. "The Army breaks you down and builds you up their way. To think their way. To brain wash you," he said.

During one of the marching drills, someone fell and the whole platoon ran over him. "They didn't stop," Lee said. "How many bruises must he have had! I thought, 'No matter how rough it is, I'm not gonna fall down.'"

They run us till you wouldn't believe, Lee wrote in one of his letters. *One or two guys have to fall from exhaustion before they stop us. One guy in front of me fell and it looked like he broke his nose because there was blood all over.*

In spite of the difficulties, many times Lee included humor in his letters. *How is civilian life? Boy is this army life ruff once in a while. We had that 12 mile march today. It was the worst my feet have ever hurt in my life. Maybe if I wouldn't be so flat footed it would help. Well anyhow I made it. They said we would have an easy week but I haven't seen it yet and it's about over. We've had to be C.Q. runners three nights in a row now. This means you only get 5-6 hrs. sleep. And you thought I couldn't get out of bed before, well it takes blasting caps to get me up now.*

And in still another letter: *The day before yesterday we ran a mile with our overshoes on, rain suit, rifle and packs. Tomorrow we throw live grenades.*

In spite of how difficult the training was, Lee volunteered for everything. "It was big shit to have a stripe on an arm, to be a squad leader," Lee said. So he raised his hand. As a result, Lee as a squad leader had no KP or guard duty in two years.

LaRayne M. Topp

.

7

Dear Barb,

Please don't get too mad because I haven't been writing lately. They have been giving us extra work to get us ready for Christmas. We are going to work all this weekend. We got our pictures taken today. I'm getting one 8x10, nine 3x5 and a bunch of others in color. They cost $21.95. We're also getting a group picture of the whole platoon. So I'll have one to give you once.

I feel like I just went through World War III. This morning we practice pugil sticks. They are the length and shape of a rifle but have big clubs on each end. I was one of the lucky 10 to be the targets. We wore all kinds of padding and football guards. The other guys practiced running attacks as if they had rifles and bayonets. After they had their fun knocking us down we then could defend ourselves. Boy was that fun. I really let them have it.

Yesterday we had hand to hand combat practice. The guy I practice with is about 230 lbs. and 6'2" but all fat. They teach us how to get our enemy off guard and get him off balance. It's just a blast to throw that guy on his ears. They teach us how to fight for keeps like breaking the enemies neck, back, legs or just smashing him. You better watch it when I see you. Ha Ha

On all classes we have, someone screws up and everyone has to do about 25 pushups. We usually do about 100 extra pushups besides the 50 or so during P.T. (physical training). I don't think my arms are getting any stronger cause it's just as hard every time. We have at least 1 hr. of exercise a day. I guess they really aren't too bad and I enjoy them. Today we had our weekly test.

Our Senior drill sergeant (the one that drinks so much and is a lot of fun) said he was in a hurry to get to town and said he would help us on it if we bought him a fifth of gin. Everyone gave money so he just went down the 40 question test and gave us every answer. How about that!

I think we might tear the barracks down tonight because there won't be anyone here to watch us. The drill sergeant said if there were girls here it was ok but we have to call him. (He was joking of course.) Don't worry. I haven't seen a girl for so long I forgot what they look like. Guess you'll remind me when I see you. I hope you look the same.

Don't write after Tuesday.

I guess I can tell you something but don't worry. It won't happen again. Last night they worked us late out in the field so we marched back in the dark. (Against regulations) Well anyhow I was in the front of the platoon. We were passing an intersection and a car ran into the rear of us. About 25 guys were hurt. 3 seriously. 3 were still under the car when it stopped. I wasn't even close and could only hear it.

It kind of shook everyone. The 40 lb. packs we always carry gave them some padding.

We march all day with that 40 lb. field pack on and at night when you take it off you sure feel lighter. It sure builds you up.

I'm running out of things to say. How much of my writing can you read? I'm a lousy speller. Guess I need a secretary. Boy you sure write some long letters. Thanks. I appreciate them.

Last night we went to the P.X. Everyone bought a big suitcase for our stuff and a couple of fifths on the way home. I think I'll just be a good kid but then again I might be dancing off that train. I think we should have one party when I get home. (How about it?)

I hope you recovered from the phone call the other night. (I'll pay you for it)

Last night one of the other squad leaders jumped out of bed and looked up yelling "who in the hell is pouring that water." Some dream.

It's really funny to see what the army does to some guys. In another platoon a guy started marching in his bed. Nothing like that happens to me I think. I don't think it's changed me at all. I guess I goof off too much to take it too seriously. There are always so many funny things happening.

Well it's time to hit the sack.

Lots of love, Lee

Lee had a leave from basic training during Christmas of 1967. He took the bus from Fort Lewis to Omaha, a 54-hour trip because his bus was stalled for eight hours due to snow in Casper, Wyoming. Lee jumped off at Columbus, Nebraska, a little over an hour from home.

The Army suspended basic training during the winter holidays, and recruits were given the option of returning home to enjoy the holiday with family and friends. At some Army posts, the event was referred to as the Christmas Exodus.

A couple of recruits went AWOL from Fort Lewis at Christmastime of 1967. "One of them said he was not coming back after Christmas leave," Lee said. "He was right."

The acronym AWOL, or absent without official leave, described a situation in which soldiers were absent from their post without a valid pass. After being absent for 30 days without the intent of returning, soldiers were no longer considered AWOL, but deserters.

During the U.S. Civil War, Army deserters were flogged, tattooed or branded. The maximum punishment for desertion in wartime is death, although no one has been put to death for desertion since 1945. Commonly, soldiers absent without official leave underwent a court-martial, or military trial, to determine guilt and punishment, typically imprisonment for 18 months or less.

Even so, by the year 1971 more than 7 percent of Army soldiers chose the possible repercussions of desertion from the Army over the life-threatening realities of Vietnam.

LaRayne M. Topp

8

Dear Love #19,

It's 1:15 a.m. and I thought I'd open my weary eyes and write a letter. I'm real sorry about not writing every day but if you were here you would understand.

We have been having night classes lately. I've been so busy and feeling sick that I'm thinking about going AWOL. Today we trained on how to crawl on our backs through wire, over ditches, logs, etc. It wouldn't have been too bad but it rained all day. The whole range is sand and clay. I wished I had a picture of the way we looked. It really was kind of funny. If you left any pockets open they got filled with mud. We also climbed through water over our heads. You probably don't believe all this but it sure is true.

Tomorrow morning we have a complete class A inspection. Our lockers and everything have to be just perfect 'cause the brigade commander is inspecting.

Once in a while things really get you down if you know what I mean and it's sure nice to hear from the outside world. It kind of gives you hope. Please don't give up hope because I don't write. I'm not much for writing letters anyhow and besides nothing too exciting happens. You probably aren't too interested in what I'm doing. I don't think I always express my feelings in my letters. It seems like it takes at least 1 hour to write a letter.

I think I'm still about the same so please don't give up hope but if you want to go with some other guy that's already through the service there isn't much I can do about it way out here. I guess it's really your choice. Maybe once I get out of this damn place things will look up. I'm counting every day (21 left).

I hope I get stationed in Texas or Georgia or somewhere where it doesn't rain everyday. I hope you can read this. I guess I should start writing something more interesting if you're still reading this.

Thanks for the one stamp but I'll need more. I don't have any way to get stamps or post cards. I'll send you some money for all expenses (like phone calls).

How is your Ford running? I suppose mine has been wrecked or burned up by now. How did you turn out with those glasses? It sounds like it's sure cold in Nebraska. Weather here was nice but sure changed for the worse now.

Did you throw all your Christmas presents away yet? I'm sure making use of the one you gave me.

We had our qualifications test on the rifle range yesterday. I got sharp shooter. I guess if you get expert you got a real good chance to go to sniper school and that didn't sound too exciting. Score keepers were informed to make sure everyone passed (in other words cheat). I guess I'll get one of those medals. Monday we're going to have a G-3 test. I guess we got a lot of tests coming up. I think it might be worth my time to study a little and get as good a grade as possible. (Boy more things to do.)

Our platoon got first this week in inspections. You really have to push the guys to get it. Morale is pretty low and we haven't been getting too much sleep.

I guess we might go to church this weekend. That would be different. I guess I might not go so I can write a letter and get my personal things done.

Next Wednesday I think is bivouac. We will be out for 3 days and two nights and there aren't any post offices in the field.

Well there I go on rambling on about my problems. Don't get too shocked over the length of this letter. I had to get up in the middle of the night so I could get a warm shower and thought I might as well stay up. I'll be dead tomorrow.

Have you been checking on my mother? You ought to go over and cheer her up for me. I wished I could be home to cheer you up. Write and tell me what's all new even if it isn't important.

Joke. Do you know why Smoky Bear's wife doesn't have any children? Answer – everytime she gets hot he hits her in the head with a shovel.
Love, Lee
P.S. You're really Love #1 not 19

A number of activities were prohibited during basic training. Insubordination, of course, was at the top of the list. Recruits were expected to refrain from smoking or using any forms of tobacco, and they couldn't be caught eating except during designated meal hours and in specified areas. Failure to perform duty, fraternizing with the enemy or being AWOL got recruits in plenty of hot water.

"We marched to the PX one time a week. We'd better not be caught with candy bars or cigarettes," Lee said. "The officers searched what we bought, and if you had it, you threw it in the trash can. Pushups were punishments. Fifty pushups when you screwed up."

Some tasks were mere routine, to teach the recruits self-discipline. At night, Lee said, they polished their boots. The next morning the boots had often dried out and turned white, requiring more polishing.

Of course, there wasn't much else to do. The recruits could see Mt. Rainier from Fort Lewis on a clear day. "That was our entertainment," Lee said. "We never got to go anywhere."

Instead, they marched.

Or they ran.

"It's surprising how fast you can run with a number 13 boot up your butt," Lee said. "It might have been harassment."

They practiced low crawls through the water under strands of barbed wire while live and deadly ammunition rocketed just overhead. With line after line of recruits dragging their bodies along the ground, the path soon became pockmarked with holes, deep holes often filled with a foot or two of water. The recruits tried to crawl around the holes, but Lee was caught in the act. The drill sergeant put his foot on Lee's back and pushed him to the bottom of the hole.

On one occasion, the recruits advanced in a forced march, trotting for miles.

"It rained all but two days while we were at Fort Lewis. It snowed them two," Lee said.

When they got to their destination, they sat on aluminum bleachers covered with frost. "We were sweated up from running and sat on the bleachers. The whole class was out there," Lee said. "Two people died in basic training. We were always wet."

LaRayne M. Topp

9

Dear Barb,

Well here is a letter from an old friend. I'm still alive. We got back from bivouac 10:00 a.m. Friday. It was a blast. We set our tents up in a huge circle about ½ mile in diameter. We set them up in the daylight Wednesday in the middle of a forest. Boy does it ever get dark. After supper it took us ½ hour to find our tents. We had to have guards out all night. I was suppose to check on them but didn't even get out of my tent for fear I'd get lost and miss out on some sleep. The Drill Sergeants and Lieutenants gave the guards a hard time all night. They shot blanks and scared them in every way. One guard threw a rock at our Lieutenant and just missed him. One guard made the Corporal show his I.D.

Thursday afternoon we had an 8 mile march at 106-126 steps a minute. That's about as fast as you can walk. We then got to fire 80 rounds of ammo through our rifles as fast as we could. That was fun. We marched about 5 miles Thursday night with 60 lbs. of gear on us and wearing our wet weather gear. Bloody murder!

We got there about 9 p.m. It was a riot trying to set up a tent in the dark. More fun is to dress. The next morning guys came out with shirts inside out and shoes on the wrong feet.

We had our P.T. test Friday afternoon when we got back. We sure were tired. I passed all the tests pretty easy but that mile run still gives me a little static. I improved 35 points from the last test. We get our final test next week. Hope I don't screw up. We also have all our other finals next week.

Sunday morning

I just got back from breakfast. Us guys found ways to get more food. I ate 4 bowls of cereal, 4 hot cakes, 2 glasses of milk, 3 pieces of toast, one bowl of hot cereal and a grapefruit. Man am I stuffed.

After church

I guess I wasn't the only one dozing in church. I think everyone was sleeping because we didn't get too much sleep last night. We had night fire. The way the army does things is ridiculous. Just because things are on the schedule we have to do it and that's the only reason. They told us to count our scores on the way down and back from the targets. The sergeants all had plans for Saturday night so they told us to get it done as fast as possible. So I filled out my score card for expert and just fired all my ammo as fast as I could. I guess we got today off.

Yesterday we had classroom all day. We had two hours on marriage advice. That was kind of entertaining.

Friday night we went to the snack bar right after supper so like a dumb nut had a malt, large Coke, and hot dog. Boy did I feel terrible.

I suppose this is sure a mixed up letter. Well it is I guess. I bet it's a real challenge to read also. Some of the guys got their orders already. They were all Infantry and a one way ticket to Viet Nam because their training is in Fort Polk. I didn't get mine yet.

If I get infantry I'm thinking about joining the Green Beret or special forces or airborne. If you're going to get shot at anyhow you might as well get paid for it.

It has been raining just about every day.

I guess that forced march is Tuesday and it's 12 miles in 3 hours. We march to a Viet Cong village.

Sunday afternoon

Weather is great. We got all the windows open. I guess we can use the day room today so maybe I can play some pool. On second thought I think I'll sleep.

Well I guess I'll sign off for now.

Lee

P.S. Be good and say Hi to everyone

* * *

"I guarded it with my life," Lee Heckman said about the M-14 assault rifle issued to him by his drill sergeant. He may have guarded his rifle so carefully because a fellow soldier happened to lose his.

Because of the recruit's carelessness, the drill sergeant made the recruit bury his rifle in the hard-packed earth. Bury it standing straight up. Four feet deep.

Then the drill sergeant made the soldier dig it back out again.

Then the soldier got his butt chewed, Lee said.

His rifle was dirty.

Lee was careful about how he referred to his weapons. If a recruit was foolish enough to call a weapon a gun, he was forced to recite a rhyme in front of the troops, with special reference to both his weapon and his penis, *This is my rifle; this is my gun. This is for killing; this is for fun.*

"The military straightened most kids out," Lee said, with its strict regimen and subsequent enforcement. The recruits of the platoon following the rules most eagerly were awarded with use of the rec room. Those who didn't, tried harder.

Basic training was good management training for the business world later on, Lee believed. He attributed his success in later life to that.

"When you're the drill sergeant with 50 soldiers under you, you have to be efficient," he said.

LaRayne M. Topp

10

Dear Barb,

Don't be too surprised that you're getting a letter. I'm not supposed to be writing. We just got bawled out for doing all our personal things before our work. We're cleaning up all our equipment to turn it in tomorrow.

I guess I've been lucking out or else going fairly good for once. I maxed the P.T. test Monday. I made over 400 points which got me in the 400 club. The highest out of 200 guys was 472 points so I guess I'm not too fat yet. I maxed the rifle range and got an expert badge instead of the sharpshooter like I thought I had.

The Drill Sergeant had a meeting today with us Squad leaders this morning for the E-2 promotion. He said we would be guaranteed E-2 if we made the G-3 test today. I'm sure I did pretty good on it (Hope).

I maxed hand to hand combat. Can't wait to get home and try some of it out.

So do you like bloody war pictures? They really don't sound too exciting to me anymore since I'm getting pretty close to see some of it myself. Well I guess that's life.

The drill corporal said I won't have any AIT but only on the job training.

Boy would that be nice.

He says Kentucky is real beautiful this time of year. I should be there Friday night.

If their Army planes are anything like their buses it might be something else getting there. I guess a drill sergeant goes with us.

We had a knife fight in the barracks today. Nothing too serious.

There is about 6 inches of snow on the ground now. It sure made it *hard on that P.T. test. Some guys must have fallen down 10 times on the mile run. The track was just ice.*

Well I guess I better finish cleaning up my equipment.

Love, Lee

* * *

An initial test of physical fitness at the beginning of basic training gave a baseline for subsequent tests throughout. To see how much the recruits improved each week, they took PT (physical training) tests. Lee could run the mile in eight minutes.

"One kid ran the mile in 4 ½ minutes in combat boots," Lee said. "He knew how to run. At the end he was waiting for us slow pokes."

Tests were strenuous.

Boy do I feel like I'm in bad shape, Lee wrote in a letter in January of 1968. *My arms are still sore from those shots and then today we went through an obstacle course. We had to climb a high tower (50 ft.) on ropes, climb logs and all kinds of goodies. We have rifle P.T. every day now. I guess they're getting us ready for the final test.*

Final tests proved whether recruits were proficient in weaponry: various types of rifles, grenades and machine guns. Recruits who passed the final physical training test moved on to bivouac (camping) and field training exercises. Exercises included nighttime combat operations with drill sergeants working against the recruits in many night operations, trying to foil the recruits' best laid plans.

Several companies often enacted simulated combat scenarios, generally at night, with intense competition to prove which company was the better trained.

At the culmination of basic training, often called "recovery week," recruits serviced or repaired any items they wouldn't be taking on to further training, plus they ensured the platoon barracks were ready to receive the next platoon of recruits.

During this time, the recruits' dress uniforms were given a final fitting and recruits practiced for the graduation ceremony while they waited for orders for their next move.

11

Dear Barb,

Well how is everything in Nebraska? I got my orders today and will be leaving Washington Friday. I'm going to Fort Knox Kentucky. There about three of us from Norfolk going to the same place and type of training.

About 10 guys are going to Fort Polk and quite a few to California.

Don't write after Wednesday cause my address will change. I'll write as soon as I can to get you my new one.

Friday night we went through an infiltration course. We low crawled 300 ft. through mud with machine guns firing 44" over us. It was until a ¼ lb. of dynamite exploded in a pit about 10 ft. from me. It kind of threw me off the ground. Anyway I'm still alive.

Monday we have our P.T. test and Tuesday we have the G-3 test. Wednesday we turn in our equipment. Some of us will ship out as early as 1300 hours Friday.

Monday night we get No. 1 haircuts again (short). They are just starting to grow out nice.

Well I guess I'll sign off for now.

Love, Lee

* * *

At the completion of basic training, soldiers were classified with an MOS, or military occupational specialty. Lee's was ground reconnaissance—and his title officially was Army Infantry Intelligence Specialist Tank Scout. His job—his MOS—was 11 Delta, or an Armored Reconnaissance Scout with the II Bravo Infantry.

Delta and Bravo stood for letters of the alphabet, with these letter names coinciding with a soldier's MOS.

For instance, II Bravo were infantrymen or ground troops. "II Bravo were grunts," Lee said. "They were the popular ones. We needed a lot of them."

12

Dear #19,

Well how is everything? We turned in most of our equipment this morning. We just got done eating and I'm stuffed. We turned in our rain suits so we stood in line in the rain for ½ hour. We got all our work done so we got it pretty easy. This afternoon we get paid, get our direct orders.

We just got back from getting our orders. My hopes just dropped about 99.9%. You was wondering if I'd go to Viet Nam, well, that I don't know but if there is any action where I do go I hope the Lord is with me.

I'm leaving here Friday afternoon and get to Fort Knox the 4th.

Well I guess I really don't feel like writing right now. I'll try to write tomorrow.

Lee

P.S. I don't think I'll get any days off. Sorry.

* * *

At the time Lee Heckman received his marching orders to Vietnam, the number of troops ordered to the country had hit its peak. President Lyndon Johnson, whose initial plan was not to win the war but to bolster South Vietnam's defenses until South Vietnam could take over on its own, raised the maximum of U.S. soldiers bearing weapons in the land of Vietnam to nearly 550,000.

The year of 1968 was the most expensive of any spent in Vietnam, with the United States throwing more than 77 billion dollars in the direction of the war effort.

The year also proved to be the deadliest for America and its allies. Nearly 28,000 South Vietnamese soldiers met their death in 1968, along with around 16,600 American soldiers. In addition, approximately 200,000 communist forces died.

The week of February 11 through the 17 in 1968 was the deadliest week of the war, a period in which more than 500 Americans were killed in action, and more than 2,500 were wounded.

During this week, the North Vietnamese led a surprise attack, assaulting U.S. forces and South Vietnamese soldiers in what became known as the Tet Offensive. This coordinated assault attacked around a hundred South Vietnamese cities and towns as well as General Westmoreland's headquarters and the U.S. Embassy in Saigon. The Tet Offensive led many Americans to believe that the enemy was stronger and better organized than they first thought and was the point at which President Lyndon Johnson decided to change his mind about continuing to escalate the war.

Consequently, the Tet Offensive became a turning point in America's involvement in the War. Prior to that, President Johnson's escalation of the war in Vietnam had divided Americans into two warring camps: those who agreed with his decision and those who preferred for the war to end.

Johnson's refusal to send more U.S. troops to Vietnam following the Tet Offensive was seen by some as his admission that the war was lost. It was seen by others as an admission that the war couldn't be won by escalation—that the cost in American lives would be a price too great to pay.

13

Fort Knox, Kentucky

Hi,

Well we got a little time this weekend so I'll scratch a few lines. It's been so long since I wrote I don't know where to start. I guess I'll start back at Fort Lewis.

I passed all the tests in pretty good shape. I made the 400 club on the P.T. test.16 out of the 50 of us made E-2. In case you don't know what that is it's a pay raise and promotion. There sure was a lot of disappointed guys.

We left Washington (in rain) Friday afternoon at 2:00 p.m. We got on a plane and got to Louisville at 3:30 a.m. It's an hour's drive from there to Fort Knox. I qualified for this L.P.C. (Leadership Preparation Class). It sounded kind of good so I decided to take it. After processing, we finally arrived at our barracks 10 a.m. Saturday morning.

The first order was start spit shining your boots. Well if you knew how my boots looked you know how I felt. Our first reaction was, what did we get into and how can you get out.

We have an inspection every morning. Everything just has to be perfect. He inspects with white gloves on. Any dust anywhere and you get demerits. If you do something outstanding you get a merit which eliminates 5 demerits. I volunteered to go over to the new class tomorrow and help them get set up. This will give me one merit. I only got 5 demerits this week. I passed today's (Saturday) main inspections with flying colors. Some guys got about 30 demerits.

There are 48 of us guys. We are set up as a company in model form. The leadership positions are rotated each day. The positions are First Sergeant, Platoon Sergeants and Squad leaders.

We conduct ourselves as an actual company would. I've only been a squad leader one day.

We will graduate Friday. We had our weekly final test this morning. I got 91 so I guess that wasn't too bad. Lots of guys failed.

When we get to AIT (Advanced Individual Training) we will have first choice for squad leaders and platoon guides. We won't always get a position but the training will help you anyway. After AIT we can advance onto Drill Corporal School and this Drill Sergeant school, or we can go to O.C.S. (Officers Commissioned School) and become a Lieutenant.

If I go overseas after AIT (which chances are very good) I should get a pretty long leave. Hope I get it 'cause it might be the last one I see.

You think my address is long well how about my M.O.S. – Army Infantry Intelligence Specialist Tank Scout. We are also called recons – reconnaissance.

I washed my clothes last night. I waited until 11:45 for the dryer and still didn't get it. I had a sleep in this morning. Until 9:15. I'm just starved because I missed supper last night and breakfast this morning because I was sleeping.

I went to the P.X. last night to see what was up for Valentine's Day. I think all the basic trainees must have got the candy already. All the cards left were for (my husband) and I didn't think that would fit in anyplace. I guess I'm going to just send you a whole bunch of lovin.' Please don't send anything but the same cause packages don't fit in too good right now.

I'm having a terrible time writing because I'm laying in bed. I guess it's only 10° outside right now. I guess it's kind of like Nebraska weather except it hasn't rained or snowed yet. All the grass is green.

I think I'll start a Beatle (hair cut). My hair is just long enough that I can comb it now.

Have a very happy Valentine's Day. I'm sending lots of love in this letter and hope you appreciate it. Be good and don't get shot with too many arrows.

Well good by "you all."
Love, Lee

* * *

During the first part of basic training, the Army put muscle on its recruits. During the second part, the Army "made a man out of you," Lee Heckman said. He went into the Academy at 160 pounds, but was 215 solid pounds when he was through.

Advanced Individual Training, or AIT, helped narrow down a recruit's specialty, and gave them specific training in their chosen MOS, or military occupational specialty.

Lee spent the initial part of his basic training at Fort Lewis, Washington, and the latter part at Fort Knox, Kentucky, incorporating AIT with a two-week Leadership Preparation Course for which he volunteered.

While at AIT, recruits were screened for the NCO Academy—the Non-Commissioned Officers Academy. The Leadership Preparation Course thinned out the recruits for placement at the Academy, Lee explained.

Before Lee went to the NCO Academy, he received orders for Germany. Those were voided, however.

Even if you were fortunate enough to be stationed in Germany, "orders didn't mean you'd stay there," Lee said. There was no guarantee.

At the time of Lee's enlistment, he wanted to be a mechanic. As the Army tested his aptitude for various jobs at AIT, he soon learned that he would be doing what *the Army* wanted him to do.

There was a shortage of NCO's in Lee's field so they offered him a place in the academy. Lee came out as an NCO E-5, or Buck Sergeant and didn't have to re-enlist, although he still had to salute the commissioned officers.

"It was progress, and I didn't have to sign my life away," Lee said. "It was available and I raised my hand. I was a Hadar farm boy," he said. "I volunteered for everything."

Lee spent 90 days at the Academy. Fifteen years of training was crammed into that short period of time, he said. "We were called ninety-day wonders."

At the Academy everything was perfect. In the footlockers were starched uniforms, but they were all for show. Instead, Lee lived out of his duffel bag, and hid the rest of his belongings under the steps.

"You could bounce a quarter on the bed," Lee explained.

Recruits ran everywhere during the entire course of training. "If you got caught walking to the PX, even on a Sunday afternoon, that was a no-no," Lee said.

Academy soldiers received training over every weapon, plus they learned about debugging mines and driving a tank. Tanks spanned 28 feet, Lee said, and weighed 57 tons, with tracks so long a tank driver could cross a river with it.

Recruits were trained using Armed Personnel Carriers. An APC was not designed to be in the river all the time, but could swim; however, Lee's was the first class to drown one. All that was sticking out, when they were through, was the antennae. All recruits got out safely, as the APC slowly sank into the river.

Consequently, discipline was swift.

One of the men who screwed up during his AIT training, Lee recalled, ended up scrubbing the inside of a dump truck—a dipsy dumpster—with his toothbrush, all the while screaming, "I won't do this again."

Recruits evaluated each other on a scale of 1-10 once a week, especially to see if they felt they could trust one another.

"We knew each other, if someone was a butthole or a nice guy," Lee said. "The buttholes were gone the next week to become a ground pounder at Viet Nam. Grunts were the most popular shortage of people."

Those who remained were willing to stick it out, as Lee tells in a letter home: *Boy is this academy murder. We just got back from running for 2 hours. We had to practice keeping in step. I had to buy a pair of paratrooper jump boots and they kill my feet. They were right in saying you have to know shorthand. They actually give you enough work for 6 people and I'm not kidding. Your appearance is extremely high standard. You must shave twice a day, put on a new polished belt buckle twice a day, have spit shined boots at all times and have a newly starched set of clothes on every day. I have about 15 sets of clothes. It costs 85¢ a set to get them cleaned. I got a $7.00 cleaning bill for last week. My boots cost $17.50. And you think you got bills?*

They say we will be in the best physical shape of our life. They are constantly on your a?? and making you do pushups. We do about 100 or so a day plus 1 hr. of P.T. and we run to all classes and everywhere in the area. After a pretty tiring day we work half the night. We must shine our boots (1 hr.), iron clothes (15 min.), hand buff the floor (2 hrs.), shine belt buckle (15 min.), 1 hr. detail, shine helmet liner (15 min.), study assignments (1 hr.), and get supplies from P.X., go to the cleaners and your personal things. You get about 1 or 2 hrs. a night to do all this. It's just a real test to see how you can do under extreme pressure. I guess they let up after 5 wks. or so. I really don't think I'll be here that long.

Lee's letters also spoke of night patrols and ambushes: *We set up actual ambushes with blank ammo. Boy it's a different feeling to have someone in your sights and let him have it. It sure feels real. We're getting all kinds of guerrilla tactics and scouting training. Monday we start our final training called the F.T. X., field training exercises. It's a solid week of this tactics, patrols, and ambushes etc. from morning until at least midnight every night.*

I guess by the end of the week you fall to sleep everywhere.

14

Dear Barb,

Got your package yesterday. It looked like it was thrown around a little but still tasted good. We had to eat them all that night because we had an inspection Saturday morning and we aren't allowed food in the barracks. I guess I got a pretty long day again. I got up at 4:30 a.m. Saturday, went to classes until noon and on C.Q. from noon until 7 a.m. Sunday or later. I'm in the main orderly room behind the First Sergeant's desk. Too bad I'm not there for good. I was just sacked out when someone from the barracks called and said Charley troop was over stealing things again. We have been having lots of trouble lately. Our Sergeant about got his head beat in one night so it's a detail for our platoon to "get" that guy. If I caught someone stealing my stuff I don't think I'd hesitate to kick his head in.

This week was real easy. We had indoor classroom Monday – Wednesday and then fired the Caliber 50 machine gun. Boy you could really tear someone up with it. They are mounted right on the tracks by the Track Commanders hatch. Friday we fired the M.79 grenade launcher. You can shoot grenades out up to 350 meters.

Next week we fire the M60 machine gun. We have to qualify with it. The M60 and Caliber 50 fire 450-550 rounds per minute so I hope I'm on the right end of it in combat.

We should be getting our orders in our 7th week. I just know where I'm going. The specialist on C.Q. with me is a real good guy in one way but he is a drug addict. His buddy just got sent to the stockades for smoking pot so he is going to quit that. He just takes every kind of pill he can find especially painkiller pills and is usually in a good mood as you can imagine. He sent me in the other room to sleep before while him and another buddy had something or other. He only has 5 days left in the service. This army can really do things to a guy.

I kind of hate the training we're getting now because there isn't a challenge to it for example. I missed all the classes on track maintenance and still maxed the test. If you flunk one of these tests you are definitely in bad shape.

It's 3 a.m. right now. In another hour and a half I'll be up 24 hrs. Guess I'd better keep writing to keep awake.

The buddy I went out on the town last weekend wants to go out again this weekend. I think I'd better sleep because I'll never catch up during the week. I've had 3 weeks of training and haven't gotten over 6 ½ hrs. sleep at a night yet. This guy that wants to go out said he never drank anything at all before he came in the Army but said he kind of has to now if you know what I mean. When he has a few drinks it eases his mind about home and everything with it but when he drinks too much he kind of feels sorry for himself or just makes him feel all the more lonely so he doesn't have to worry about drinking too much. The same applies to everyone in the service I think. Boy when you're on C.Q. and just set in a chair for hrs. and hrs. you sure have lots of time to think. Well skip it.

I'm kind of getting in a bad mood like I was the night before I left so I'd better sign off.

Love, Lee

P.S. Thanks again for the cookies

* * *

Near the end of AIT, Lee and fellow recruits took part in a two-week bivouac. They lived in the bushes and slept in pup tents. Each man had one half of a pup tent, and most had a buddy with a second half of a tent to share with. Invariably, the number of the men would not be an even number.

"It would always come out odd. Always there was one guy with half a pup tent, sleeping under half of a tent. It was always raining, and there you were, laying under half of a tent," Lee said.

As the men slept in the rain, after a few days many men were on sick call. One day, the sick call people were marched into town—a distance of 12 miles. No one was at sick call the next day, Lee said.

The young men at AIT tried to mix a little fun in with the grind whenever possible. They soon tired of picture shows, and went instead to ½ price nights with 25 cent mixed drinks. Vodka and Tom Collins were their favorites.

"Today I can't stand the cherries," Lee said.

It was 20 miles from Fort Knox to Louisville, Kentucky. One weekend, Lee and a buddy left Fort Knox for Louisville in a 1966 Chevelle convertible. At every stop light, Lee's buddy behind the wheel squealed the tires from Fort Knox to Louisville.

"There were hot chicks in front of us in a car and we chased them," Lee recalled. "No harm from us; we were just playing."

But at 3 a.m., Lee and his buddy looked up and saw a sign for Chicago, 179 miles away.

"Woo! We got to get back," Lee told his buddy.

Lee had a girlfriend back home, he said, so no drugs, no sex. Beer was as far as it went. Consequently, he taught a friend from Idaho—a Mormon—to drink beer. The officers gave them lists of area bars and told them where *not to go*, so of course those were the first ones the recruits headed to, Lee said. One evening, they stayed at the YMCA, with Lee's friend hanging onto the power line, puking out the window.

They went to the Rats Killer bar, a German bar on base at Fort Knox. As they downed a beer, they flung the bottle over their shoulder.

A man in the corner was bleeding.

"It's time you left," the bartender told them.

They skedaddled from the bar.

At times, Lee also considered absenting himself from basic training as well, as his letters show: *I'm pretty fed up with this course and am seriously thinking about shoving it. There was 60 in our class. Two are in the hospital, one on bed rest, and 25 are putting in quit slips Monday. I think I'll drop out too. I sprained my left ankle and it's about an inch or so bigger than the other and I pulled a muscle in my stomach. We have to do pull ups before we eat and I swear my guts are pulling apart. Guess I should go on sick call. They never did let us build up for the P.T. They started right out with the max exercises. Last Wednesday the Sergeant got mad and made us do 60 eight count pushups. My arms were so stiff I couldn't bend my arms.*

Other than these slight difficulties I'm having a great time. Ha Ha
Even so, Lee stuck it out.

LaRayne M. Topp

15

Hi,

Well don't get a heart attack because you're getting a letter from yours truly. I guess it's been so long since I wrote a letter I might have to learn how again, not that I ever did know how. Like I told you a long time ago I'm not much for writing. I thought I better not call again because you would be tired of talking to me. Also it's kind of expensive but don't worry about that cause I'll get that bill squared away with you when I see you.

I hope my letters make a little sense. I don't ever read them over before I mail them because I can't read my writing.

I just got back from Louisville but I'll tell you about that later. I'll start telling you all my great experiences of the last couple of weeks. If you aren't interested just stop reading.

I survived bivouac in great shape. It got up to 80° every day. It was a little muddy the first couple of days but all turned pretty nice. We played war games all week. One platoon was mounted on tracks and the other were on dismounted patrols. We used blank ammo and had real battles.

It kind of shakes a guy to pull the trigger on an M14 or M60 machine gun with a man in your sights even with blanks.

I can see being a scout isn't the most safe job. It kind of makes you think to realize those will be real bullets in the near future. They say that you don't have to worry about the bullets with your name on them but the ones that have "to whom it concerns."

Some of our orders are coming in. Saturday they read off 23 guys' names who are going to Viet Nam and one who is going to Alaska. Not a bad ratio huh?

Last night the sergeant said the reason we are in recon is because we scored high in mechanics and map reading. We are so called hand picked. Ft. Knox is the only recon training center in the world.

Getting back to bivouac we did have lots of fun. We just about burned a hole in our tent, buried a track in a mud hole and got lost in a forest. We had a night compass course. Our group made it in good shape. The next group, the guy that had the compass got lost and the rest of the group made it in by themselves. Boy did they ever tease him. We only spotted one snake. Kentucky is full of copperheads and rattlers. One guy rolled a jeep in a river also.

One night out there our captain kind of stuck his foot in his mouth. The First Sergeant's daughter was out there with him. She is blonde, 20 years old and kind of good looking. Anyhow he saw us goofing off and used one of his very greatest 4 letter words real loud without thinking. He sure got embarrassed.

Last week a tank blew up. One guy died already and the other two are in critical shape with burns. A bad round of ammo blew up and started everything on fire. I talked with a guy that said he was suppose to go in that tank but got changed. He said he seen the guys jump out all on fire. He said it could have been him. I doubt if it will be in the paper.

To do something different 4 of us went to see what Louisville is like. Well you just wouldn't believe it unless you see it. A normal Saturday night is like Norfolk during the centennial or a carnival. Sidewalks are so crowded you have to walk on the streets. You name it and it's got it. There is a show on about every block and 5 bars to a block. There must be 2 or 3 girls to every guy but don't worry. I maintained my cool. The guy with me is also married.

We went to see the show, "The Graduate." It was real (I mean real good) good. I doubt if they will show it in Norfolk and if they do some parts will have to be cut out. We stayed at YMCA. We had a pretty good time. We brought a little beer and stuff to our room.

They also had a dance there. A buddy of mine drank a pint of whiskey straight and went out of his mind. He was real funny. He about fell out of our 3rd floor window and then he went to his 4th floor window and was hanging out of the window on a telephone wire with only his shorts on. We then put him to bed after he barfed. Before that we went down to the dance, sat down and 4 girls came over to see if we would dance. We said no and went back upstairs to have a beer. When we came back down they were gone.

People are a lot more friendly here than in Norfolk. The guys that want dates just stand on corners and a girl will come and pick you up or ask what you're doing. But don't worry! OK? Us guys just stuck together and didn't need any women to keep us entertained.

Well I guess I ran out of all those good looking pictures. I've got guard duty tomorrow so I guess I better start spit shining my boots. I don't have to walk guard but I am a commander of the relief. I take the guards back and forth to their posts. On our eighth week we have our big inspection. A Brigadier General inspects everything. So we got lots of work to do. Thinking of you, Lee

* * *

On the day of Lee's graduation from the NCO Academy, 34 were pictured on the graduation picture.

"We started with 100," Lee said. "That's how many were left."

Lee ran 26 miles on the day of his graduation. He ran some, then tested, he explained. He would answer questions on the training they'd been given, and then run again to the next location, a half mile or a mile at a time. It was the final test.

Lee with sister Diane

Everyone graduating from NCO ended up in Vietnam, Lee said. He graduated as a buck sergeant—E-5 after only nine month's experience, skipping E-4, and was turned loose as a drill sergeant. A promotion equaled a pay raise. The NCO Academy graduates who went over to Nam, went so as an E-5, Lee said. It was one pay grade over a Specialist.

Lee was offered E-6, but turned it down. The promotion was the next step to Vietnam. An E-7 was the king pin running the platoon.

"I didn't want to be in charge," Lee said. "I didn't have enough experience, knowing where I was going."

He was working beside an E-6 who'd been there 18 years.

"There was some resentment," Lee said. "You had to cut the

mustard."

On the first day Lee reported as an assistant drill sergeant, the E-6 told everyone else to report as well.

"They all flew out of the barracks," Lee explained. "It took five minutes. The drill sergeant had them do 25 pushups. He had them report again. This time it took two minutes."

He turned to Lee. "Okay. Sgt. Heckman, we expect nothing less."

"So I got to be a bad ass drill sergeant too," Lee said.

16

Fort Knox, Kentucky
April 11, 1968

Well here is another letter from an old G.I. I really don't blame you if you quit writing because I never write back. As you have found out already I'm not the best letter writing and I'm getting worse. I know you don't understand why I don't write and I can't really explain. Home and you seem to be a million miles away. If it wouldn't be for your letters I would lose contact with civilization all together. I guess I'm not the type that expresses feelings in a letter. The feelings I have right now about the Army I don't like to express. I guess I just kind of like to feel sorry to myself and keep my problems within me and not write and tell everyone. I suppose this sounds pretty dumb but I can't think of anything to tell you about the future except I'm graduating Friday, my address will change Saturday and I will not get a leave.

Lately morale has been pretty low, not too many people are pleased with their orders and everyone is pretty hard to get along with. So see you aren't the only one in a bad mood once in a while.

Last night was the first time we got out of the barracks for 2 weeks. A few of my buddies and I went down and bowled a few games and then went to a real swinging place and tried to drown our troubles.

After everyone was half in orbit a few fights started. One cool cat in our company whom nobody likes really got pounded. One guy came up to him and hit him 3 times in the face. He was bleeding all over. After I left someone threw a beer bottle at a cook and hit him in the head. (More blood) I was pretty good and came through with few scratches.

We got our 8th week inspection behind us now. You think you houseclean well all 100 of us in our company have been housecleaning for the last 2 weeks. I never went to bed before midnight and if we got caught writing letters or goofing off we got more details. I swear a few more days of that and I'd go out of my tree.

Please wait and keep writing if you really want to. Also wish me good luck because I think I'll need it. I should have time to write tomorrow night and I might be in a better mood.
Love, Lee

* * *

In 1968, during Lee's tour of duty, the importance of basic training was stressed to young recruits, under the assumption that 90 percent would be heading to Vietnam. Even so, many of them hoped for a tour stateside, or a stint in Germany, perhaps. Anyplace but Vietnam. In one of Lee's letters home, he stated that fellow recruits had their orders, all to the infantry with a one-way ticket to Vietnam. Lee expressed an interest in joining the Green Beret or other special forces.

"If you're going to get shot at anyhow, you might as well get paid for it," he wrote.

"*We just got back from getting our orders,*" Lee wrote to Barbara in one of his last letters in basic training. *My hopes just dropped about 99.9%. You was wondering if I'd go to Viet Nam, well, that I don't know but if there is any action where I do go I hope the Lord is with me.*"

But one day Lee knew his future plans for sure. He could no longer anticipate the worst news; he'd been handed it. In preparation for overseas service, Lee recalls receiving 26 shots in one day.

"They ran us through like cattle," he said. Blood was running down the arm if a vein was hit in the process. Some of the men passed out.

On the way to Vietnam, Lee flew out to Oakland, California, where he met up with an old Mormon buddy, as Lee refers to him – a friend who missed his own wedding ceremony because of the aftereffects of his bachelor party the evening before.

Lee's Vietnam-bound plane refueled at Alaska, and it was there that the soldiers enjoyed their last stateside drink. They were all minors, but none of the bartenders—knowing where the soldiers were heading—asked for identification.

"We soused down every drink we could," Lee said. "The soldiers on the way to Nam drank enough so that when they got on the plane they would either pass out, throw up or go to the bathroom.

"It made the trip quicker," Lee surmised.

When soldiers were dressed in uniform they received first class treatment. They flew military stand by, and never got bumped.

"There was probably some old lady who got bumped and she sat on the runway when we flew," Lee said.

En route to Vietnam, Lee's unit landed in Japan. On his return trip, Lee flew home by way of Hawaii.

"I can say I've been to all kinds of places. I don't have to say I didn't get out of the airport."

LaRayne M. Topp

17

November 2, 1968

Dear Barb,

Well how is everything in the good old USA? Did you have fun on Halloween? I guess we are 1 day ahead of you here.

If Mom talks to you about what I wrote please don't tell her everything I tell you because she would only get worried. OK?

Well as you know we left Oakland (California) Sunday afternoon. We stopped in Alaska for 45 minutes so Dave and I had a last stateside beer. We then flew to Tokyo, Japan. Our next stop was to be Bien Hoa (near Saigon in Vietnam) but it was being hit with mortar and rockets at the time so we landed near Saigon (at Tan Son Nhut) until it cleared up.

Since we gained a day it was Tuesday morning when we got to Bien Hoa. We then took a bus to Long Binh which is the replacement center. Boy it was terrible there. Hot and dirty.

I met a buddy I had in basic. Kind of surprised me to see him. At Long Binh, Packer and all my other buddies caught up with me.

Thursday we arrived at our unit which is the 1ˢᵗ air mobil cavalry. I'm at An Khe. This is my unit but I'm still not assigned to my troop yet. This is just another replacement station.

The night before, Charlie broke in, blew up an oil station and landed 3 mortars. The oil line has been burning ever since. There are about 30 Charlies inside our perimeters so after 7 we are restricted to our building. 4 men were killed during the attack.

After we get processed here we have 4 days jungle training at Camp Evans (which they never did arrive at) which is 30 miles south of the D.M.Z. I guess we go on live ambush patrols and stuff. After this our unit is moving south around Long Binh.

Well I guess that's all and still no address yet. Don't write this address cause I'll never get it.

Love, Lee

* * *

Looking out the airplane window, as Heckman's plane circled Saigon, he received a quick introduction to the War in Vietnam as the landing strip was bombarded with mortar and rockets.

"Fourth of July now is pretty dull in comparison," Lee said. But at the time, seeing the fireworks on the landing strip below was exciting. "We were kids," he said. "We were excited."

Instead, the plane landed near Saigon at the airport of Tan Son Nhut until the shelling cleared. The United States used Tan Son Nhut as a major air base during the Vietnam War, stationing Army, Air Force, Navy and Marine units there. From Tan Son Nhut, the soldiers traveled by bus to the Replacement Center at An Khe, a type of suburb of Saigon, in Binh Long Province.

The soldiers settled down with their duffel bags in buildings that Lee described as old hog sheds, to wait for orders and to learn where in Vietnam they would soon be stationed.

"I suppose they were barracks," Lee said years later. "The hog barns had open windows, if there were any windows, and it was 100 degrees in there."

Lee and fellow soldiers waited ten days for their orders to be cut, answering roll call several times a day. Subsequently, it was at the replacement center where Lee learned the value of fire extinguishers, but not because of the heat or any blazing fires.

"I didn't think we'd ever get so desperate as to drink warm beer," he recalled. But after sitting around all day, waiting for their orders, they found that if they sprayed warm cans of beer with fire extinguishers they soon had cool beer. "There was always a shortage of fire extinguishers," he said with a grin.

As Lee was contemplating his tour of duty in Vietnam he wore the Shoulder Sleeve Insignia of the 1ˢᵗ Cavalry Division of the U. S. Army. A black horse's head on the upper right corner of a yellow, triangular shield was worn proudly by its soldiers. The colors of the shield were symbolic, dating from the Cavalry's establishment in 1921 after the Army instituted a permanent cavalry division. At the time of the Vietnam War, no longer a conventional infantry unit, the division served as an air assault division, using helicopters as troop carriers.

At the beginning of the war, in July of 1965, the division began its deployment to Camp Radcliffe at An Khe, Vietnam. For the next five years, the division's chief assignment included perfecting tactics and doctrine for helicopter-borne assaults on the enemy. The unit went on to earn the first Presidential Unit Citation presented to a division during the Vietnam War.

In 1967 the division re-deployed to Camp Evans, north of Hue, Vietnam, and during the 1968 Tet Offensive, was involved in recapturing Quang Tri and Hue. The unit moved on to relieve Marine Corps units besieged at the Khe Sanh combat base in 1968. In the autumn of 1968, the First Cavalry Division relocated to An Khe, northwest of Saigon, and in May of 1970 participated in the Cambodian Incursion.

The bulk of the division was withdrawn in April of 1971, but its 3rd Brigade served as one of the final two major U.S. ground combat units in Vietnam, leaving finally for home in June of 1972.

Casualties suffered by the 1st Cavalry Division in the Vietnam War included more than 5,400 killed in action, and more than 26,500 wounded in action. As one of the most famous and most decorated combat divisions of the United States Army, the 1st Cavalry Division was one of the first units to make its presence felt in Vietnam.

"The 1st Cavalry was pumped up like Nebraska's Big Red football team in the 1970's, right next to God. It was impressive to be on the winning team," is how Lee Heckman described the 1st Cavalry Division. "We were pepped up. We were kings. Everyone liked to fly."

LaRayne M. Topp

18

November 4, 1968

Dear Barb,

Well guess you about forgot about me by now but I'm still here. It's Saturday afternoon and I'm still at An Khe with no address. It sure would be nice to get some letters.

We got here Thursday and I guess we'll be here for a week because we are going to take our jungle training here instead of at Camp Evans. After this training we will move south to the Mekong Delta around Saigon and clear and build a new base camp.

We got hit again about 5:00 this morning. A mortar hit a big oil tank about 2,000 meters from us. It burned all morning.

Well it's now a bright and sunshiny morning (Sunday.) They had a movie last night but it didn't interest me so I just laid on my bunk.

All the buildings have tin roofs and the top half of the sides are screen and the bottom half wood. They are real cheap. There is no running water or indoor bathrooms. To find a bathroom all you have to do is go outside and smell and you can tell if there is one within 2 blocks.

The last 2 days it's been fairly cool because it's been cloudy. It even gets cold at night. We had a real quiet night last night except for outgoing mortars and frogs.

I met a Spec. 5 from Utah and we have been sneaking out of all details together. You see we know we won't ship out for a few days and as soon as you're done processing they put you on details. So we just go to the rear of the line and then sneak off to the P.X., snack bar, Red Cross club, or barracks. We have been doing this ever since we got here.

I guess we get combat pay for October even though we were here only a few days.

Oh ya they tried to put our group on K.P. yesterday but E-5's don't have to pull it so we took the day off while the others had it.

Well do you have it figured out how many days I have left? I leave here 26 October 69.

Do you think you can get me a way little calendar about the size of a picture so I can mark off the days? I have one for 68 but need one for 69.

Did you get the map?

Boy I don't know about the shower situation. I think the water is dirtier than I am. They were out of water for 3 days. Drinking water has chlorine in it.

Well be good and tell everyone hi for me.

Still here, Lee

* * *

They were someone's son or brother, nephew or grandson. They were altar boys, 4-H'ers, baseball players or captains of the high school basketball team before War changed them. Parts of men died in Vietnam, and forever afterward they awoke in the night in a cold sweat, screaming. Some of them quit breathing for good.

At the tender age of between 18 to 25, young men and a percentage of women—just kids really—made up the preponderance of those who ended up in Vietnam. As they left the states, naively excited about the possibility of adventure, nothing could have prepared them for what was ahead.

Lee Heckman was no exception. Just as nineteen-year-olds in the States cruised main street, Lee's crew flew downriver, known to take potshots at alligators and elephants. As they flew over some of the French settlements they discovered that some of the women went around topless.

"We'd fly around there quite a little," Lee said, until the day the men in the settlement took out their weapons and shot in the air to chase the choppers away.

During the Christmas truce, Lee's unit was under orders for a cease fire. Both sides called a truce. Lee and his fellow soldiers weren't

content with that. Instead they flew over Vietnam and peed on the jungle below.

"We showed them," Lee said, laughing at the absurdity of their actions.

Typical of young men living anywhere, Lee's unit kept a little pet. *He's a banana cat or fox or something,* is how Lee described the pet in a letter back home to his mother. They named the cat Agnew after their first sergeant whose first name was Agnew.

Some colleges ask for pen pals so we gave his name to them, Lee wrote. *We can't wait until she asks for his picture. He is about 6" tall. About the size of a cat. He loves bugs and already had his first combat battle with a dog.*

Young men in Vietnam lived in every way as far apart from their counterparts in college back home as night is from day, as Janis Joplin is from Wolfgang Mozart, as a shiny new Rolls Royce is from a rusty, beat up jalopy. Even so late night discussions led them outside of their immediate situation in Vietnam and to, as Lee wrote, *Mars, space, religion, and the twilight zone.*

LaRayne M. Topp

19

November 5, 1968
Sgt. Lee Heckman
1ˢᵗ Cav Division (airmobile)

Dear Barb,
    Well today is the 5ᵗʰ. I met a Spec. 5 and we are the only 2 in our barracks. We have been doing as little as possible or in other words nothing. We haven't been on a detail yet.
    I think our jungle training starts the 7ᵗʰ and it's right here at An Khe. So I guess it will be about the 13 before I get to my unit.
    I guess we get mail 7 days a week. It takes 4 days to mail a letter and the same time to receive one.
    I hope my mother doesn't have too big a party because I just sent her $513.00 the other day. I hope she puts it in the bank for me. I'm kind of thinking about buying a car over here. You can get a Volkswagen for about a thousand, a Plymouth Roadrunner 383, 4 speed for $2,755, and I think a Chevelle for about $2,500. We can get them directly from the factory here and have them waiting for us in the states.
    Stan and I walk down to the P.X. about twice a day and get a Coke and Stan goes girl watching. I seen 96 and 98 piece china for $36.50 – $45.00. Is that cheap?
    Yesterday Stan bought a case of beer and then found out he couldn't get any ice so he had to drink it warm.
    It's been cloudy just about every day and not getting too hot.
    I hope days are going faster for you than me.
Lots of love, Lee
    The base camp at An Khe was the size of a small village, but it was taking on more than its share of fire. According to Lee Heckman, it was the target for around 1,300 incoming rounds a day, although—mercifully—not every day. Mortar shells were fired, one after another,

from surrounding trenches where North Vietnamese snipers were safe—for a short time, at least—from exposure to U.S. forces.

U.S. soldiers didn't have to strain very much to hear the *plop* sound indicating a mortar had been hurled from its short, stumpy launching tube, arching overhead in its deadly downward spiral to blast into pieces an unprotected soldier, mess tent, barracks, machine gun post, or ammunition dump before the U.S. soldiers could detect the mortar's delivery point and return fire.

There was little to do at that point and little time to do it except to duck, perhaps, and pray. Even so, religion was never brought up in Vietnam, Lee Heckman said. One guy out of 100 wanted to go to church, in spite of their fear, anger or depression.

There was no place to hide, Lee explained. Even when soldiers were in bed, there were air strikes. There were no guarantees; there was no way to get away from it. Even in the relative safety of the base camp, U. S. soldiers died.

How can anyone who has never lived in a war zone relate to that feeling?

You get used to it after a time, Lee said. But....

"It's an eerie feeling, not to be safe. The only thing you can do is to wait until your year is up."

20

November 8, 1968

Dear Barb,

Well we completed our first day of jungle training. We just had classes on the helicopter, military justice, pot, grass, VD, etc.

We now have our M16 rifles and ammo. Yesterday we went to a rifle range about 5 miles outside the perimeter and set it up. It's been real quiet around here and nothing happening.

I seen the show "The Bible" last night. They had church services for us this morning.

I've never tasted such bad food in my life as we get at the mess hall so we went out and got a T-bone steak. It cost $2.50 but was worth it.

I just heard I might ship tomorrow instead of finishing training.
Well be good.
Love, Lee

* * *

Lee had spent a considerable share of his time in basic training learning the ropes of ground reconnaissance. He assumed that when his plane landed in Vietnam he would utilize his training and commit his days to armed reconnaissance. Instead, Lee ended up in aviation—air reconnaissance.

Lee in front of H13 Loach

"That's what they gave me," Lee said. "That's more or less the book end of it."

And it was a good thing, Lee said. It was cool up in the air, hot on the ground. Plus, he didn't have to walk. He began his tour of duty flying in a light observation helicopter—an H13 Loach. That was his chopper.

A larger, more heavily equipped attack helicopter, a Cobra helicopter known as a gunship, flew immediately above the Loach, with crew members reading maps and watching the backs of the men in the Loach, while delivering fire to the enemy.

Utility helicopters with room to deliver troops were called *slicks*. Medical evacuation helicopters, or medevac choppers, returned from the battlefields with scores of wounded.

Although Lee began as an observer, he ended up as a door gunner on an observation helicopter. Through a process of seniority, observers branched into gunners, who doubled as crew chiefs.

"We had scouts who flew secret missions, to see what was in the area. We flew to the hot spots. We flew to the fire and put it out. It was our job to get shot at and get out of there. We were not supposed to stick around and get in trouble. We weren't the infantry. We were not designed to be John Wayne."

"We were just three people in a helicopter," Lee said. "We couldn't save the world." But if necessary, because of their vantage position, they stayed on the scene and continued firing until more help arrived.

"It was dumb to bail out if someone was shooting at us. We'd slap the guy silly. We knew exactly where he was at because he was shooting at us," Lee said.

It was a natural thing for Lee to be a door gunner, he said. Gunners shoot left-handed and Lee is left-handed. He sometimes flew with one foot on the chopper's skids—or landing gear—balancing precariously on the skids to fire to the right or underneath the chopper to the other side or immediately below.

Typically, Lee flew without the benefit of a seatbelt. At one point, Lee's chopper was radio'd that something was flopping from the chopper.

"It was my seat belt," Lee said. "I never wore it. Some other guys were roped in."

Lee fired from the hip, without using sights. As an observer, Lee's M-16 rifle replaced the M-14 he used at basic training. The M-16 had become the standard U.S. rifle of the Vietnam War by the late 1960s, and was used by the observer. As a door gunner, Lee used an M-60 machine gun, firing somewhere in the neighborhood of 450-500 rounds a minute. Lee sometimes shot 10,000 rounds a day.

Choppers were designed such that a torque gauge was added to each chopper's engine because manufacturers put only so much power to the engine, Lee said. Rotor torque readings, or red lines on gauges, told pilots how close they were to flying to design limits before overtaxing the gears.

Sometimes, Lee said, when they were "in hot stuff," they would shoot until the barrel of the machine gun got red. Once red hot, the machine gun never shot straight again.

"When things were getting hairy you did what you had to do. When we were getting shot at and the barrels were hot, we said screw the red light, and kept firing. We wanted to get out of there."

The most stressful job in Vietnam was the door gunner, Lee was told after the war. And the number two spot was the medic.

Lee explained it this way: "Some had good jobs, some had crappy jobs, some had worse jobs, some had worser jobs.

"Veterans don't compare notes about how bad they had it. It's not a bragging thing, because someone always had it worse."

Loaches spent time as flying bait, while the soldiers inside tried to sort out who was the enemy and who was friendly. Friendlies and the enemy looked alike, Lee said. French were friendly, and the South Vietnamese working with U.S. soldiers were friendly.

Viet Cong, or the North Vietnamese Army, were not friendly.

It was a simple matter for Loach crews to find out who was friendly and who was not. It was their job to draw fire. When they were shot at, it was easy to deduce the holder of the weapon below was not friendly. The choppers flew over the jungle at tree-top level, so their occupants made easy targets.

Their job was to be shot *at,* but not to shoot at the enemy, Lee explained. However, the H13 Loach had room for four people. The two seats in the front were occupied by a pilot on the right and the observer on the left. One of the back seats—the one at the right—was occupied by a door gunner. Occupying the fourth seat was a box of ammo. With the ammunition on the seat beside him, Lee fired from the back right door.

"It wasn't my job to decide who was friendly," Lee said. "I didn't run the war; the pilot was the boss. The pilot said, shoot or don't shoot. Otherwise it was a free fire zone, which meant shoot at anything that moved."

Lee and fellow crew members soon learned not to fly down the same river, following the same path every day, as the enemy would be alerted and set a trap.

"They saw us every day, and figured they could snag a couple of us," Lee said. One day the enemy strung a cable, high across the river.

"The pilot saw the cable in time, thank goodness," Lee said, and he pulled up before the chopper collided with the cable. "It would have been a bad day."

21

Dear Barb,

Well how is everything in the world? Boy did I have a ruff day.

I got up about 6:45, ate, laid back down until about 11:00 and the other guys in our hooch decided to make rooms. So we now have our own rooms. I built a large cabinet so I now have a place for all my stuff and can lock it up.

I put in my own electrical wiring but am short some connections. Do you think you can send me a couple of things. I need a connection that screws in the socket where the bulb is and has plugins on it.

Hope you can understand all that. If you send it in a small package and it's under 5 lbs. you can send it air mail and I'll get in 4 days. Anything bigger goes by boat and takes 30-40 days.

As for details the only thing I have is C.Q. which I guess is about every 2 weeks. I don't have to pull guard or KP as an E-5.

As for work during the day I won't start until I take my flight physical. I guess another Spec. 4 and I will fly to Sook Bien tomorrow for it.

After that we fly missions. A mission will last about 2 hrs. We have 10 choppers and about 25 of us guys so it will be anywhere from 0-8 hours a day work. They usually work it out so you get every other day off. Only in extreme emergency do we fly in the dark. They have only gone out once in the last 5 months at night so I guess there won't be too many night missions.

My section leader and I went to the P.X. today and got 5 cases of beer. He said that makes the 15th case he bought this month.

Well guess I'll sign off. Let you know how I turn out on my physical and trip. Love, Lee

Once the United States became involved in the war, a whole new round of words were incorporated into the vocabulary of Americans seated in front of their television sets as nightly news anchors spoke of body counts, kill ratios, and search and destroy missions. Sandwiched between the laughter brought forth by comedians Lucille Ball and Red Skelton, and the aw-shucks humor of Andy Griffith and Gomer Pyle, replays of jungle warfare continued to set the stage for growing unrest in a war a world away.

Television listeners began to squirm in their comfy recliners.

U.S. soldiers, however, were provided front row seats in the fight against a well-supplied Viet Cong army. The Viet Cong were experts in setting deadly ambushes and elaborate booby traps. And once the ambushes and traps were set, they could escape by following escape routes through a complex network of underground tunnels. For U.S. soldiers, the majority of them just 18 to 25 years old, they were suddenly light years away from the entertaining gunfire of *Gunsmoke* and *Bonanza* they'd enjoyed listening to only a few months before. For them, hunting for an elusive enemy—let alone leasing their fire power on them—proved daunting.

Once determining that its formidable enemy hid its activities under triple-canopied jungle, U.S. forces unloaded a colorful array of defoliants on large areas of the Vietnam countryside. Rainbow herbicides (Agent Orange and its less famous cousins Pink, Green, Purple, Blue and White) removed foliage as it burned jungle leaves away, especially when used in combination with napalm bombs.

But napalm didn't stop with tree leaves. This burning, jellied gasoline lit a torch to everything it touched, burning human skin to scorched, red skin and charred, black remains. When unleashed on its victims, its firestorms brought about heat stroke, dehydration, suffocation, smoke exposure and carbon monoxide poisoning—and at its worst—deformed and baked corpses.

High numbers of confirmed kills—on either side of the war effort—gave television viewers a sense of how the war was progressing. High numbers of confirmed kills—on either side—either provided listeners with a sense of relief at how proficiently the U.S. war machine was mowing down the enemy, or depending on their point of view, a sense of horror at the same thing—how proficiently the U.S. war machine was mowing down the enemy.

As for Lee Heckman—an integral part of the U.S. war machine—individual body counts could be observed from his tree-top view from the door of his helicopter, much like Americans noted the number of deer left dead on the side of a roadway.

"The numbers always got fabricated," Lee Heckman recalled. "One could turn out to be five, or five could be one, vice versa. Changing numbers could make it sound like we were doing better at winning the war."

LaRayne M. Topp

22

November 14, 1968

Dear Barb,

Well I finally got to my unit. I'm at Quan Loi which isn't on the map but is about 1/16" above An Loc on the red line.

Yesterday when we flew down from An Khe we had engine trouble and landed at Cam Ranh Bay for a couple of hrs. It's a big R and R center. People were all over on the beach, water skiing, etc. I kind of had to hitch hike to my unit.

I stayed in a small base camp Phuoc Bihn last night and got a ride on a chopper (helicopter) with a major. So now I'm finally sitting on my own bed and able to unpack my stuff.

I guess I'm in the best unit in Viet Nam. Everyone kind of respects the Cav. The reason it's so good is because it's airmobile (able to relocate permanently within a relatively short amount of time). It can move any place in Viet Nam in 12-36 hours and have a complete new base camp cleared and built. It has 420 choppers.

My job (you'll never believe it) is driving a chopper (Lee used the term "driving" as an armor-trained soldier) *and observing. I also will be a door gunner. A Warrant officer is the real pilot but I must know how to fly also in case something happens to him and I guess they let you do most of the flying.*

We go out in our chopper (on missions) and have a Cobra chopper over us for security. A Cobra is a gun ship with rockets, mini guns, machine guns, you name it it's got it. Nothing here has more fire power. I'll draw another $55 flight pay also.

The ground around here is red clay like in Kentucky and <u>real dusty</u>. Everything just has a layer of dust on it.

As for track vehicles they <u>don't have any</u> so most of my training didn't do me much good. I think I'll enjoy being on a chopper. There is no walking at all.

Well they don't have showers set up yet so I guess I'll have to get along best I can.

My address is the same except the APO number. If you mailed any letters with that older APO number I haven't gotten them yet and might be a while.

So write and be good.

Love, Lee

* * *

Quan Loi stood as an Army supply base surrounded by rubber trees leftover from an old, French rubber plantation, located about 60 miles north of Saigon near the town of An Loc, the capital of Binh Long province. An Loc was about 20 miles from the eastern border of Cambodia.

"This is where I lived," Lee said about where he worked and made his home. "It was a small world."

When Lee Heckman arrived at the Quan Loi base, the 1st Cavalry had just been relocated there. The Cavalry was mobile enough it could relocate within a short period of time to hot spots as they flared up.

"We had inklings where we might go next, but it didn't always happen," Lee explained.

At Quan Loi, the men were housed in tents, and just three doors down from Lee's tent, the mess tent had been bombed, its canvas roof battered and torn. Nearby, Lee stayed with the non-commissioned officers, instead of sleeping with the rest of the soldiers in his unit.

"We were wheels," Lee said. "We had our own tent, a hooch."

Lee slept on a cot with a mesh of mosquito netting spread over the top. His cot stood on an old rug covering a dirt floor.

"And we were the elite ones," he said.

Showers were a block away. Lee said he came back from the showers dirtier than when he went because of the blowing, red clay dust. He was glad he wasn't there during the monsoon season.

23

Sgt. Lee Heckman
Viet Nam
November 15, 1968

Dear Barb,
Well how is everything in the world? I guess I better get back to writing.
Well I flew 3 missions yesterday and one today so I got about 8 hours flight time in. Every 25 hours you get a flight medal.
The first two missions we didn't spot anything. You see we fly at tree top level and between trees. It's all circus rides put in one. If trees aren't wide enough to go straight through you fly sideways. These choppers are small and can fly in about any way. I just about lost my stomach my first mission. We scout ahead and look for anything and everything like trails, bunkers, people, etc. These choppers are nothing but great.
Well yesterday, the 13 for you, we ran into a little trouble and got broke in fast. We got in more action since they moved south. I thought I'd really get scared but I didn't. Anyhow we got down into the action and medavaced one of our men out. I guess they put our names down for an award for going down and getting him. Their chopper was hit by an APG round and blew the rear tail about 300 meters away and then crashed into this river. The other two crew members didn't make it.
Well don't get all worried because I kind of enjoy being in there and doing a good job that counts. I guess I like a ruff job. It's really great working with a good bunch of men. It's well known that we're the best here.

We're now getting cavalry hats. They're like a cowboy hat except it's black and got a yellow rope on it. It's real sharp. Can't wait until I get mine.

Boy we get some great food here. I don't think I've lost a pound.

Did you hear anything about U.S. troops killing 3 people and wounding 12 others in Cambodia. Well that was us scouts. They were N.V.A. – North Vietnamese Aggressors– that just jumped the border and thought they were safe. Well they weren't. There has been all kinds of hell raised about it because Cambodia is supposed to be a neutral country and an international law or something was broken. But see if anyone fires at us we have the right to fire back so they said they fired first.

Well I got my door gunners clearance today and got my M60 machine gun.

I get $55 extra (per month) for being a crew member now.

The mail situation around here is bad. I guess we only get mail when they feel like bringing it to us. But write anyhow. OK.

Well be good.

Love, Lee

❋ ❋ ❋

The fact that the Vietnam War was fought on Viet Cong home turf complicated the fighting for U.S. soldiers. The Viet Cong could attack the enemy and then simply melt back into the countryside— their countryside.

In the middle of hot missions, U. S. soldiers weren't allowed to cross over the border dividing Vietnam and Cambodia or Laos; they were to fight the enemy in Vietnam. But sometimes, if their Loach was being shot at and they were hunting down the enemy who was responsible, they would tippy-toe across the border, Lee said.

The *Ho Chi Minh* Trail ran alongside Vietnam from north to south through Laos and Cambodia, countries that were officially neutral and exempt from U.S. forces. Cut through malaria-ridden jungles for about 1,700 miles, the trail encompassed a mesh of interlacing foot paths. With groundwork laid in 1959, these paths were eventually developed into a secret road system for truck traffic bringing food, weapons, ammunition and an estimated one million North Vietnamese soldiers to battlefields in South Vietnam. Convoys traveled at night under cover of darkness. In addition, the enemy was adept in the act of camouflage.

During the First Indochina War, a tunnel system was begun throughout Vietnam for its citizens to use in one of two ways: to both hide in and survive. Initially set up to hide wanted individuals and then families, the tunnel system extended its reach to hide supplies, guerrilla units and even whole villages. Excavated by hand, the dirt moved by shovels and woven baskets, the interconnecting tunnels were reached through well-hidden entrances. When the Vietnam War began, this system of tunnels was employed by the Viet Cong, and continued to expand in direct relationship to U.S. firepower.

Some tunnel systems were small, utilized as underground base camps or shelters for villagers and soldiers to hide in when the enemy searched a village. Other systems were large, extending for thousands of miles. Others, even larger, expanded over the years until they became quite elaborate, incorporating twists and turns, different levels and rooms, with plans for air circulation and water drainage. Whether large or small, they were extremely difficult to locate, as the openings were concealed in brush and grass, hidden inside bamboo thickets and among tree roots, buried in rock piles, or disguised as support for other village buildings.

"The VC were superior in that they had bunkers, caves and tunnels," Lee said. Hospitals were built underground, and rumored to be ten stories deep. "We found lots of caves. They were tunnel people."

We didn't understand that bunker system they had. We couldn't even flood them out, but we threw lots of Willie Peas down in them, he wrote.

When Lee served in Vietnam, hand grenades were oftentimes taken away from scouts serving in positions like Lee's. "You have just three seconds after you pull the pin," Lee said. "Evidently, some scouts didn't throw it quick enough and got shrapnel from his own grenade. Some were evidently too dumb and hung onto it too long, so we were given Willie Peas, like a hand grenade only filled with white phosphorous."

One of the incendiary agents used in grenades, white phosphorus burned at a temperature of 2,800 Celsius or 5,070 Fahrenheit, with a poisonous, lethal nature. "We used the heck out of Willie Peas," Lee said, tossing them into caves to clear the enemy. "It's a chemical, so if you got it on your hand it wouldn't quit burning. It would burn clear through to the other side unless you smothered it with mud. So we gave it to the enemy, throwing it in holes, caves and tunnels."

LaRayne M. Topp

24

Dear Barb,

Well it's 10:45 and it's my day to fly but we don't have a mission yet so I thought I'd write. I hope we get a mission because I'm going up as a gunner. Maybe I'll get to really tear things up if you know what I mean. The other day we burned down a complete village but there wasn't anyone around. I guess the VC left the night before.

We got about 8 women around here to rake the yard, sweep the floors, etc.

I guess I'll fly about every day for a while because I need the experience.

Yesterday we shot 2 deer.

N.B.C. has been here taking film so if you see any choppers with cross sabers on the nose and a square on the side you know it's us. If you see any ads in the paper about the 1st Cav or anything else of interest please send them to me.

Oh by the way I haven't gotten any mail yet. Guess I'll have to quit writing also.

My hair is pretty long now and about completely blond.

Have you figured how many days I have left? Well can't think of anything new and everything is pretty quiet around here.

Be good, Lee

❊ ❊ ❊

"It was a fast way to get broke in," is how Lee described his first experience in action in Vietnam.

His letter, told in a few, simple words—as always—tells of the mission while downplaying the danger of the situation. Well yesterday we ran into a little trouble, he wrote, if you would call rescuing a downed chopper amidst a barrage of fire, a "little trouble." Talk of the peril was sandwiched between that of flight medals and cavalry hats, and ending with crew pay and the mail situation.

Flying over one of the rivers threading through the central highlands of Vietnam, alongside high mountain ranges and plateaus surrounding Ah Khe, Lee and his crew spotted a downed chopper. One of the men from the crashed ship was standing in the leech and snake infested river, waving at the helicopter overhead. The two men with him were dead.

As Lee held off the attacking North Vietnamese snipers with rifle gunfire, the pilot maneuvered the Loach through thickets of trees lining the river, down to where the frantic man waited. As the helicopter hovered overhead, the soldier reached for the landing gear and clung to the skids for his life, his body dripping with water and slimy with mud.

Steam rose off of the jungle floor, shrouding the rescue as the helicopter rose higher, the man dangling beneath.

As any Nebraska farmboy turned military soldier might describe it, "We fished him out of the creek," Lee said. "He latched onto the skids and we got him out of there."

"You can't kill yourself going to rescue someone," Lee warned. "When an aircraft is down, sometimes it's suicide to help, but in panic things don't play out as good as they should and rescuers will go in and get killed," Lee said.

"But, I'm still here."

A request for a commendation medal for Lee follows:

Department of the Army
Headquarters 1ˢᵗ Cavalry Division (Airmobile)
6 January 1969

Award of the Army Commendation Medal for Heroism
Heckman, Lee A., Sergeant United States Army Troop B, 1ˢᵗ Squadron (Airmobile), 9ᵗʰ Cavalry

Awarded: Army Commendation Medal with "V" Device
Date action: 14 November 1968
Theater: Republic of Vietnam

Reason: For heroism in connection with military operations against a hostile force in the Republic of Vietnam. Sergeant Heckman distinguished himself by heroism in action on 14 November 1968, while serving as a serial observer during a combat mission in the Republic of Vietnam. When a helicopter was downed by enemy fire, Sergeant Heckman's aircraft immediately flew to the location of the crash. Upon spotting the lone surviving crew member hiding near a river, the pilot hovered his helicopter over the man's position as Sergeant Heckman placed a devastating volume of suppressive fire upon the enemy emplacements. The downed soldier was safely rescued as he clung to the helicopter's skids and was flown to a friendly location. Sergeant Heckman's fire-power covered the lift out of danger. His display of personal bravery and devotion to duty is in keeping with the highest traditions of the military service, and reflects great credit upon himself, his unit, and the United States Army.

LaRayne M. Topp

25

Dear Barb,

 Well I guess I better answer your letters since I got 4 already plus the package. They're postmarked the 10, 11, 19, 20.

 To answer a few questions as for a Christmas present for my mother, knickknacks for the walls, pictures, floor mats for her car, earrings – ? I really don't know what she needs.

 It's kind of cool today about 65°. So far the temperature is just right, not too hot not too cold. I guess in December or January it gets to 120° though. I've got a pretty good suntan already. Kind of different than your weather there. The reason it's so cool I guess is because of that typhoon. I guess we're suppose to get 50 m.p.h. winds.

 Last night I was Sergeant of the guard. They changed it from C.Q. to that. I was in charge of 4 bunkers which had 3 men in each. If they saw anything they called me on the radio and I had to report it. I was on a real high tower and had a front row seat because between 9 and 10 a whole company of NVA walked into one of our ambushes about 400 meters to our front.

 Artillery shot flares out there made it about as light as day. About 3 camps around here cut loose with their artillery and then about a dozen cobras each carrying 72 rockets plus thousands of rounds of mini gun ammo let them have it and then they called in an air strike. (Actually, Lee called in the Artillery.) It was just like the 4th of July.

 I don't know if you know what a mini gun is but it's a machine gun with 6 barrels that puts out about 3,000 rounds per minute. Machine guns look sharp at night because every 4th round is a tracer. It leaves a red streak in the air so you can see where the round hits. When they open up with all *the guns you can just see red streams through the air. Oh ya each cobra has 4 of those mini guns.*

Anyhow after that was over the rest of the night was quiet. There were 4 of us on the tower so we each only had to stay up 2 hours apiece. So I got off yesterday and today.

That China I saw was at An Kai and I'm now at Quan Loi. We don't have China in this P.X. yet. In a few months or so I'll be back up to An Kai for my R and R and could get it then or else wait until I'm in Japan for my other R and R and maybe get it cheaper yet.

And as for flying the helicopter I pretty well know how to do that. The only time we would really have to fly is in case something would happen to the pilot so we don't have to be experts at it, only know how to land it which is really the hardest part.

As for me to parachute I don't because all our work is in the air. You can see about 100% more in the air than down in the jungle and if we get shot down it wouldn't do any good to jump because the big blade would cut you in half as you went through it. Unless the tail is shot off the rotor blade will continue to turn and you can usually land in pretty good shape like the day before yesterday another one of our choppers was shot down. It was hit in the windshield, gas tank and engine but no one was hurt.

You really don't have to worry about crashing as much as you have to worry what's waiting for you down there.

I hope you were right when you said you like to hear what I'm doing and don't worry. Really us guys in the scouts get to see more action because we're out looking for it. We're in a pretty hot area now and we usually find lots of things.

Did I tell you one of these nights when it's good and dark we're going to bomb the shithouse down across the street because of evident reasons? Last week we dug two trenches a foot deep and a foot wide on the road in front of us to slow down traffic. It worked real good until the Sergeant Major drove by and didn't slow down. Anyhow we now have them filled back in.

Our steak fry went over real good and the next night the mess hall borrowed our equipment and had one for everybody. As for smoking you girls think that's something well at least you didn't have pot like the guys had at our party.

I'm glad you're counting the days. My buddy here just got a 84 day drop so he could go back to college and said it was no big problem. You can

get out up to 90 days early from your E.T.S.
  Thanks much for the goodies
Love, Lee

* * *

Lee carried this well-worn map with him

One of the main problems for U.S. soldiers during the Vietnam War was locating the enemy. As some said, "Nobody knew where anybody was, and the maps were old."

Existing maps were often hopelessly outdated; but nevertheless, maps and knowledge of map reading were essential when it came to locating the enemy, evacuating wounded soldiers, or knowing the precise distance between the enemy and friendly troops when the weapons were loaded.

Military maps were vital in showing the lay of the land into which soldiers were headed. Major terrain features displayed on the maps included valleys, ridges, depressions, hills and saddles. Seven basic colors or their combinations were used to pinpoint buildings and woods, railroad tracks and roads, rivers and coastlines, lakes and elevation.

Map readers had to thoroughly understand the differences between angles of true north, grid north or magnetic north, and also grasp four-digit, six-digit, eight-digit and ten-digit grid coordinates spelling out exact locations. The higher the number of digits in the grid coordinates, the more precisely map readers were able to determine a location.

Lee's knowledge of map reading served him well one evening as he was placed in a watchtower as the Sergeant of the Guard.

"I was excited about it, but it was really a stupid place to be," Lee said later. "If there were incoming rounds, where do you think they'll shoot them?"

Guards had been posted around the perimeter of the camp as an entire company of North Vietnamese walked into U.S. ambushes. Artillery response on the ground, plus a dozen cobras in the air with their rounds of ammunition lit up the night as if it were day.

With all the firing going and rounds of machine gun fire including tracer ammunition, the sky—with red streams through the air—looked just like the 4th of July, Lee wrote.

Because the enemy was firing at the perimeter, Lee called in the artillery.

Using grid coordinates, Lee knew where to fire. He called the first round plenty far out so he was sure not to hit his own men—several 100 meters. Far enough away to keep the U.S. soldiers safe, and also far enough—or close enough—to annihilate the enemy before the Viet Cong reached the camp itself.

"Then you walk the next rounds in," Lee said. "The first round is very scary. You hold your breath. You don't want to drop a round on your own people. And if there's no more fire the enemy is dead or gone."

26

Dear Barb,

Well I guess I'll bust on and write you a letter. I've had a couple of beers so don't expect too much. I went to Saigon Sunday and enjoyed the sights. Goofed off all day. It reminded me of Italy with all the stands along the street.

I managed to get a fifth of Sloe Gin and a quart of Seagrams – so we had a steak cookout last night and I no longer have the fifth. Boy was I sick today. I slept all afternoon. I'm flying tomorrow. Our scout platoon got a real good month in January. We got 90% of the action (kills) in the division. We got put in for a situation. We already got one for valor. Don't really know if you're interested or know anything about this stuff. Do you want me to send my awards your way? I don't know if you'll be proud or scared so I'll let you tell me. Ha. Ha.

We got gooks right outside the perimeter tonight so they're pouring artillery in around us all night. Not much sleep I guess.

Oh ya on the tapes. I sold my tape recorder. You sent me a 4 track tape and I had a 2 track recorder so it didn't do me much good so no sweat. I sent a few hundred along with a buddy who is going to Hong Kong and he is going to get me a large 4 track. It will be a couple of weeks before he gets back so hold up on the tapes. I'll give you a report then.

You know I've been thinking about you all day. You'll have to try and convince me more on all that love you got stored up. When I get back you probably won't even remember me. You see I got a lot of loving to catch up on also but you probably won't accept it and treat me like a stranger. You'll just write more about all the loving you're going to give me and get me convinced and feel good.

Why don't you pick a car out for me to buy? I think I'll get a helicopter for transportation.

Well guess I'll go to bed. Wished you would be in bed here with me but guess we wouldn't get much sleep. Right!! (How is that?)

Love, Lee

* * *

To get from point A to point B, air reconnaissance choppers flew at treetop level at about 100-125 knots. That's comparable to 115 or 145 miles per hour. Choppers flew forwards, backwards, straight up or straight down, Lee explained. When they landed on the ground after a flight, Lee and his crew would spend some time pulling out tree limbs that were wedged between the helicopter's skids.

"Tops of trees are fluffy," he said.

Lee and fellow crew members had had to crouch over to get into the Loaches they flew in—with good reason. One day a crew member forgot, and the propeller hit him in the head, splitting it open.

"He got a haircut, dumb butt," Lee said. "We kept telling him to duck down!"

Lee's chopper was the most crashable of the Army air craft, meaning riders *could* survive if the ship went down. The oldest chopper they flew was only three months old. The rest had all crashed, Lee explained. Consequently, the choppers didn't break down; they were all too new. Pilots and crew didn't experience mechanical trouble very often.

On one occasion, however, the motor on Lee's ship locked up. They were 1,000 feet in the air, with no parachutes. Lee had taken his training in the armored division, not the airborne, and had been trained to auto rotate if the motor ever locked up.

The auto rotating maneuver depends on the skill of the pilot for maintenance of air velocity through the ship's rotor, with the lift provided purely by aerodynamic forces after the failure of the helicopter's transmission to keep the chopper on a slow but steady descent.

"The sheer pin kicks out and you float down," Lee said. "But you can't change your mind once you start down. You just say, 'Oh shit! This looks like a pretty nice place to land.' If it turns out to be a bad place, there is no power in the chopper's engine to change your mind. You just know you're had!"

Fortunately, Cobras kept track of the smaller air reconnaissance ships. In addition, Vietnam is a country the size of Florida, so help could come to downed ships with the assistance of radio communication.

"If you're shot down it's like when the fire whistle blows here in the states, and they send help," Lee said.

LaRayne M. Topp

27

Dear Barb,

Got your letter tonight and I'm truly sorry if I sounded like I was mad at you. I'm not.

It's just that I have been very depressed. I lost my best buddy the other day. It's real hard to take I was talking with him and an hour later he was dead. I pray it went fast for him. It really makes you wonder whether it's all worth it. Well so much for that.

Today I went down to Squadron to take my flight physical. About time since I've flown over 3 months. We scouts get an additional $65 because of our job. I thought I was blind but you know what. I still have 20/20 vision. I had to get x-rayed and everything.

Oh for the tapes why don't you wait and I'll send you the reels since I can get them so cheap. And besides I don't have another recorder yet. I got the camera but haven't got any flicks yet. I'll try it out tomorrow.

I traded my quart of Seagrams for a case of steaks and we had another pretty good party.

Have you heard any news about the Cav moving back to the states?

Your letters do cheer me up and I appreciate them. Too bad I don't have exciting news to talk about. Well be good.

Love, Lee

* * *

When Lee Heckman served his tour of duty in Vietnam he was only 19 years old. As with other young men his age, he felt he was invincible.

"It was always the other guy that got hurt," Lee said "We were never scared in our domain with an M-16 or an M-60."

When serving as an observer, Lee used a lightweight assault rifle, an M-16 with an ammunition clip, replacing the M-14 he used at basic training. The M-16 had become the standard U.S. rifle of the Vietnam War by the late 1960s.

When acting as a door gunner, Lee used an M-60 machine gun using belt ammunition, firing from the hip, without using sights. Machine guns were fired from the shoulder, hip or underarm position, and were difficult to aim without support because of their weight. For this reason, soldiers often lightened up the stocks so they were easier to manage.

Machine guns, with their chains of bullets, fired at the speed of 450 to 500 rounds per minute, sometimes firing 10,000 rounds a day. Typically, tracer ammunition was included in every fourth or fifth round of ammunition, its colored fire an important tool in following the direction of fire.

Before the development of tracer ammunition, gunners relied on seeing the impact of their bullet to adjust their aim for the next time they pulled the trigger. Tracer ammunition, or tracers, contained a small pyrotechnic charge so as bullets ignited upon firing, the composition in the base burned brightly, making the path of the bullet easy to follow.

Conversely, when the enemy used tracer ammunition—more than likely U.S. stolen ammo, according to Lee—a brightly colored charge followed their fire as well. On those occasions, Lee could tell when tracer ammunition was headed straight for him.

"It was fun to see the 4th or 5th round tracer going out, but never fun to see it coming at me," Lee said.

LaRayne M. Topp

28

Dear Barb,

Well here I am listening to golden oldies on the radio and trying to think of something to write about.

Today I am recovering from a hangover. Boy I really got tanked up. I finally made it to bed about 1:30 in the morning. I'm not flying for a few days so I can recover from my wound. Ha. Ha. I'm just fine.

Hope the army didn't let mom know or she will sure worry.

Today was payday for me so I guess I can afford to buy some film now. Wished my tape recorder would hurry up and get here.

I think I'll take my R & R in April or May and go to Hong Kong. I'm talking my buddy into going with me if possible.

My old Platoon Sergeant stopped drinking but sure is having a beer tonight and just couldn't stand it any longer and had one with us. And to think he even quit for 4 whole days. Ha. Ha.

Got a letter from your mother last night. She told me all about you so now you'll have to try and get her to confess what she all said. Good luck!

The picture is of a Cobra. It's the helicopter that covers us on our missions. Those are the rockets on the side. You can also see the jungle (I hope).

Well keep planning the future and tell me what you got in mind.

Boy these golden oldies make me homesick.

Well be good.

Love, Lee

When Lee needed a part for a weapon he traveled to Saigon, the capital of South Vietnam. He flew to the city and traded with vendors at the city's black market.

It was a simple task. Lee needed parts, he passed the word, and the word traveled up and down the vendor network until the suitable part was located.

He gave the vendor five dollars, and both were happy.

Oftentimes, Lee was unable to get the part from the United States. In an ironic twist, the Vietnamese vendor probably stole the part from the U.S. Army, Lee explained, and Lee bought it back.

"Somewhere along the way the parts get stolen; that's the reason they're cheap. A lot of our equipment ended up in their hands," he said.

The Viet Cong had good guns, Lee explained, Russian weapons and weapons stolen from U.S. military branches.

Choppers were made out of aluminum and glass with scant protection from Russian weapons, bullets or shrapnel, Lee said. Air ships were kept as light as possible, and their manufacture was a decision between two evils: durable construction material that made the ship heavier and more impervious to weapon fire, or lighter, swifter ships that weren't as safe. Because air reconnaissance soldiers were fired on from below, most were wounded in the butt or legs. To increase their chances of survival, crew members in choppers often sat on their flack jackets instead of wearing them.

Lee stole a 12" x 12" armor plate to sit on. "If I had to, I could squeeze my butt cheeks on to that little plate," he said. "I didn't share it. I stole it; it was mine. It fit my butt very well."

He never loaned it to anyone, because if he had, he never would have gotten it back.

29

Dear Barb,

Well it's 10:00 and we just got back from the flight line. We had to clean the place up. Other than that I had yesterday and today off. We found a 50 gallon barrel cut in half with legs welded on it so we're going to have a steak cookout for the platoon.

We're going to send someone to Saigon and get about 100 lbs. of T bones. And of course we'll have plenty of beer to go with the steaks.

I kind of fixed up my room a little. I spent $12.00 on plastic stringers and mats to go on the walls. I also got a large mat for a rug. I painted my cabinet blue and built a gun rack beside it. Guess now all I need is a few more pictures of you for my cabinet. Hint. Hint.

Yesterday I got up at 7 and ate breakfast and then laid back down and slept until 12:00. Ate again and went to the P.X. and got a haircut, shampoo and all that good stuff. I then got a case of Bud and a case of Millers. One guy in our tent had 3 cases and a sergeant had 2 cases so we had a pretty good time last night.

The other day I went out as a gunner but didn't see anything but bunkers and huts filled with rice so I had lots of fun throwing Willie Peas and burning everything. Willie Peas are white phosphorus grenades.

We also reconed around two gunships that were shot down. They were really tore up. One landed in some trees and a tree came right through the cockpit. I don't know how bad they were hurt. The other gunship had bullet holes all over and there was blood all over but no one got hurt too bad. We got some real hot areas around here like that.

As for the women they work around here you see men don't work over here. The women do all the work and make the living. What do you *think about that?*

We just got 56 lbs. of Swiss steaks and we are going to cook them tonight. There is 23 of us so we're each going to put a dollar apiece in for some beer.

Well I guess I'll go to chow.

Be good, Lee

* * *

Surface-to-Air Missiles or SAMs were lightweight, guided missiles designed to shoot down aircraft from a stationary position on the ground below. They contained a system to guide missiles toward their target.

"Your headsets would go beep beep when you're in the track of a missile," Lee said. "The pilot would get hissy pissy, very excited, and would maneuver, zig and zagged, to get out of their path."

When fighting became more intense than the Loach/Cobra team was equipped for, reinforcements were called in, and oftentimes those reinforcements included Arc Light bombers to take out an entire area.

"When it was more than we could handle they would send the rockets in," Lee said.

Begun in 1965, Operation Arc Light, as it was known by its code name in the military, supported ground combat operations in Vietnam. The deployment of heavy Stratofortress bomber planes to an area provided air support, assisted by ground-controlled radar. Using 750 to 1,000 pound bombs, B-52 strategic bombers, carrying almost 30 tons of concentrated firepower, disrupted enemy troop concentrations in jungle areas.

"Put 15 of these planes together and they could take out an area ½ mile by 1-2 miles long. All that's left behind is craters and tree stumps. It was the ultimate way to get rid of problem areas that kept flaring up," Lee said.

One of Lee's letters tells of a typical "flared up" week as a gunner in Vietnam, when things seemed to go wrong simultaneously. When fellow soldiers crashed and burned around him. When four holes were blown in their chopper and the pilot was hit. When, in a tight situation, when both the observer's and the gunner's weapons jammed.

30

Dear Barbie,

Well what's new back in the world? Is it still snowing? How is your Chev running? How is work? Talked to my mother lately? How are your folks? Do you still love me? What do you think about sex? Would you like more pictures of over here? Do you want some real gross sex pictures? Are you still going to get a stereo even if I get one?

Well now you should have something to write about.

Our CO. put out the rule that you can only fly a max. of 6 months (or 100 confirmed kills. No one had ever made it an entire year). So I've got 2 ½ months max. left. My Platoon Sergeant said tonight he was going to get me out sooner if possible. He said I seen enough stuff. So maybe I'll be a Supply Sergeant or something.

Well keep building all that loving up because I'm doing the same.

Love, Lee

* * *

In Cambodia, Lee and his crew polished off a few of the enemy on the Ho Chi Mein trail.

"We got lost. We didn't read the map right. We were just following orders," Lee explained. As a result, their pilot received a talking-to from his superiors.

"Just don't do it again," the pilot was told.

Lee and his crew were also told not to take prisoners. They confiscated enemy weapons, but they didn't take prisoners. However, on one occasion Lee and his crew took two prisoners. Only two.

"They just showed up bleeding," Lee said. "They were just kids. Scared, young kids."

The two young Viet Cong wouldn't give U.S. troops information, so Lee and his crew took them up in a Huey.

It was a bumpy ride, Lee said. They took the young men high in the air, blindfolded them, and then flew close to the ground. While only a few feet above the ground they kicked one of the prisoners out. For all the other young man knew, his buddy was dead.

"The other one started talking right away," Lee said. "Turns out he knew English. It might be a war crime. But I don't know how you'd get people to confess without persuasion."

31

Dear Barb,

Guess I'd best write you a letter since you think I write other people more than you.

Had a real exciting day today. Got in a real good fire fight. Of course yours truly came out ahead. Went out 4 times and got shot at every time. We didn't get hit once though (Lucky huh?)

Business has been real good around here lately. We had 2 platoons of NVA surrender. We captured a recoilless rifle, 30 caliber machine gun, ammo and lots of other goodies.

I might just get famous yet. We have had several newspaper reporters here lately and have my name, home address, etc. Even one from England.

We've been partying up pretty good lately. The other night a sergeant got so drunk he barfed 4 times and then passed out and fell in it! Last night another guy passed out outside and they found him the next morning just sacked out. You really have to do something for entertainment once in a while or your nerves will get the best of you. After being in the Scouts for a while your nerves are either shot or you just don't have any.

I now fly with Mr. Burt. He is a real cool guy. He just turned 21. The only reason I fly with him is because he is crazy. Not really but he flies that way. You just wouldn't believe some of the things we do. You know me – try anything once. Anything for a kick. We haven't ever got anybody to fly with us that won't get sick. Today the guy barfed all over. Of course we flew just about straight up about 1,000 ft. and then nose dived straight down.

He can also just about fly sideways. Gravity holds all the equipment from falling out. He also likes to fly about 100 knots at tree top level and at the very last minute go around or over the taller trees. We literally scared the ....it out of our observer today. Fun.

I'm thinking about selling my recorder and getting another better one. But it costs $134. So I don't know yet.

Can you check what a Polaroid 210 Instamatic camera costs. At Gibsons I think it costs $39. Here it costs $42 and it will take me 3 months to order it. So if the price is right get with my mother and she will get the money out of my account and get it. You can hint to her about an early birthday present or something. Anyhow maybe I can get you all a few more flicks if you want them.

Oh as for the women of course they got some real good looking ones over here. About 90% have VD or something like it. My old Platoon Sergeant went to An Lock the other day and has been giving himself a shot of penicillin every day for about a week. I know he was up to something. The dirty old man him!

Did I tell you last Friday I was a courtesy police for the day. That evening I had to be the bouncer at the L.M. club. I got all the beer I wanted so they about had to carry me out.

I didn't hear about the 15 choppers blowing up in the Mekon Delta but we work there all the time also.

I'm not flying quite as much now. They might get my number if I fly too often, huh?

When you ask me how things are going I really don't know how to answer you. All I can say is I'm still here and OK so far.

One of the sergeants here got a Dear Daddy letter so he got a 2 week leave to go get hitched. He said he probably wouldn't but she is only 15 and getting hitched is better than going to jail.

Well can't really think of much more.
Love, Lee
P.S. Thanks much for the care package
Sgt. Lee Heckman

* * *

At the time Lee Heckman set his feet on Vietnamese soil and his butt in the seat of a helicopter, Americans were dying in Vietnam at the rate of around 100 per week. Some men were killed going for a drink of water, while completing an everyday chore or going to the outhouse. Some men died trying to save their comrades from enemy fire; others were known to throw the body of a dead comrade on a live grenade to save themselves, bits of blood and body tissue landing on their helmet, their shoulders, their face. Soldiers died in the heat of battle, on the ground, at sea or in the air.

Sometimes the thin slices of aluminum and glass stretched between the framework of a chopper weren't enough to save a door gunner from a bullet with his name on it, driving up through the floor, shattering the glass or bursting through the open doorway.

If a pilot ejected as his plane was crashing and he parachuted down to enemy waiting below, guns cocked, bayonets drawn, the pilot's destination upon landing might end up being the Hanoi Hilton, a prison holding U.S. prisoners.

Sounding as if it might be a resort hotel, the Hanoi Hilton was anything but. Called the *Hoa Lo* Prison in Vietnamese, named the Hanoi Hilton by captured U.S. prisoners, and described as a *fiery furnace* or *Hell's hole* in some translations, the prison may have been a toenail's hold closer to hell than its guests could have ever imagined.

Built in the late 1880s, and designed to restrain Vietnamese prisoners—political prisoners in particular—the prison was located near Hanoi's French Quarter. U.S. Prisoners of War who were held there endured miserable conditions for days, months, even years. Food was often withheld, poor as it was. Conditions were fearful and unsanitary, and might even be described as subhuman.

Pilots, frequently in poor shape at the time of their capture, told stories of horrendous proportion. Methods of torture were designed to break the will of the prisoners: soldiers were beaten, held with rope and iron bindings, and thrown into solitary confinement. Prisoners, shackled by their ankles and hung upside down, were flogged until they passed out. Prisoner's elbows were strapped with heavy wire behind the back, with the wire pulled taut until shoulders were dislocated. Americans were interrogated and tortured with the anticipation that one day, one day soon, they would give in, give up military secrets, and overturn their allegiance to the United States.

LaRayne M. Topp

32

Dear Barb,

How is every little thing in the world? We have had a little excitement here as usual. One of our ships got shot up real bad. They're going to junk it out. The pilot had a bullet cut the side of his boot open but didn't scratch him. The gunner wasn't so lucky though. He got shot through the foot and back of his right leg. Guess he'll be OK. Nice R & R in Japan for a while.

Hunting was real good for me yesterday. I shot an alligator about 6 ft. long. And 18 cows plus a real large bull. We kill all livestock so Charlie can't use it.

How are you doing on that picture? Send me a copy.

Today we started building a lounge or bar on our hooch. When I get a camera I'll take some flicks of it if you won't mind the bad language on the walls. We got all tanked up in the process so I laid down an hour to recover. I guess I'm in good enough shape to write a letter.

When you tell me to be good you'll have to keep in mind we don't do anything that's good over here. We're all mean nasty professional killers.

So much for the bad stuff.

Hey what's this bullshit you <u>still think</u> you love me and don't think it's any use to think of your future. Well listen here kid I'll be home before long and you better start planning.

As for the TV and stereo you could use the money on other things besides I'm going to order a large tape recorder and stereo here. Do as you want though.

Well be good and take care of yourself.

The first sergeant, anxious for his time of service to run out, often let Lee make out the flight lists, deciding who would take on a flight mission that day. Another job the sergeant gladly gave up was the identification of dead bodies.

Dental records and dog tags were used to ID bodies but it was much simpler if people like Lee could name the dead men once they were returned, lifeless and bloody, from the battlefield. If no one could positively ID the bodies, the gruesome task became the responsibility of the personnel in the morgue, and they were both careful and deliberate in their assignment.

"It would be terrible if someone was told their husband or son was dead when he was really alive," Lee said.

As Lee made out the daily flight lists he noticed there was seldom—if ever—anyone in his unit who wore glasses, was married or was religious. However, one of the men who came to join Lee's unit stood out. He was both married and religious.

"This guy read his Bible," Lee said.

Soon after the new soldier arrived in the unit, it was Lee's job to wake him up at 6:30 one morning to fly. By 8:00 a.m.—a mere two hours later—Lee was also called upon to give positive identification of his torso. The tragic news had to then be relayed to the soldier's wife and family.

Lee told the story in his typical fashion. "He had no arms, no legs. He had a head, but he was burnt to a crisp."

Lee and his crew members walked from their hooch almost every day to the flight line on the red dirt roads that cut across the base, a distance of less than four blocks. En route, their path took them by the morgue. On especially hot days, the sides of the morgue tent were up, and the dead were laid out on tables, awaiting identification.

A deuce and a half truck—a large dump truck—was used to bring in the dead, crammed with lifeless bodies stuffed into poncho liners which made up the men's survival gear, part tent, part body bag.

One of the dead men stretched out on the tables was the unit's mess sergeant, shot by a fellow soldier who didn't like the food.

So accustomed were the soldiers to the sight, "Boy, they sure got a load of them today," they might say as they made their way to the flight line.

"We just walked by," Lee said quietly, perhaps defensively. "I didn't have to go in. I wasn't like I had to go in and say good-bye to anybody."

Nevertheless, soldiers were scantily compensated, no matter how many dead bodies the soldiers walked by, and no matter how closely bullets whistled by their head. Pay was based on a soldier's rank, plus entitlements. These entitlements were based on the work completed throughout the month and were added to a base salary. Extra pay was awarded for such things as housing allowance and uniform maintenance. It was also distributed based on a soldier's actions: flight pay, parachute pay, and hostile fire pay, for example.

As an E5 buck sergeant, in Lee's case he received an additional $65.00 per month for hostile fire pay—a magnificent sum to get shot at, is how Lee explained it.

Because after all, Lee Heckman had little to be concerned about up in the air. His letter back home says it all: *You really don't have to worry about crashing as much as you have to worry about what's waiting for you down there.*

LaRayne M. Topp

33

Dear Barb,

Why don't you send me some of your snow. It's sure hot here. That's why I kind of like to fly because it's always cool up there. I'm flying tomorrow. Let me know if you got my awards. I should have some more here by next month. I imagine you'll probably laugh at them and throw them away but when you're finished with them please give them to my mother so she can put them with the rest of my papers.

I borrowed a tape recorder and were listening to your tape. It's outstanding.

Did you ever get to see my new little nephew yet? Tonight at midnight Tet starts.

Well they need someone to take someone's place to fly now. Write more next time.

Love, Lee

* * *

The beginning of the Tet Offensive coincided with *Tét*, the Lunar New Year as celebrated in Vietnam. Traditionally accompanied throughout the war by a seven-day truce, in 1968 *Tét* was ruptured by a coordinated attack by communist forces, including both the North Vietnamese Army and the Viet Cong, breaking January's truce.

The Parrot's Beak, an area in Cambodia located only 30 miles from Saigon, was used by the Communists as a base of operations for the Offensive, with funeral processions used to smuggle weapons into Saigon. It had been a simple task for North Vietnamese forces to enter the cities, mingling with civilians returning home for *Tết,* Vietnam's main holiday.

At half past midnight on January 31ˢᵗ, North Vietnamese forces launched the massive, surprise attack, beginning at Nha Trang. In addition, more than 100 South Vietnamese urban centers were struck, along with General Westmoreland's headquarters and the U.S. Embassy at Saigon.

One of the cities, the capital city of *Huế,* was hit with the fiercest firepower, leaving thousands of unarmed *Huế* citizens massacred and 80 percent of the city in ruins.

During the week of February 11ᵗʰ through the 17ᵗʰ, the record for the highest U.S. casualty toll during one week was set, with more than 500 Americans killed in action, and more than 2,500 wounded.

Phase II of the Tet Offensive, also known as the May Offensive, Little Tet or Mini-Tet, struck 119 targets throughout South Vietnam, including a recurring attack of Saigon.

In March, angry U.S. ground troops retaliated, rampaging through the tiny hamlet of My Lai where they massacred more than 500 Vietnamese civilians, ranging in age from infants to elderly.

News reports of the Tet Offensive fired a public outcry against the War back in the States, later fully ignited with reports of the My Lai Massacre, which had been buried from public knowledge for more than a year.

34

Sgt. Lee Heckman
December 1, 1968

Dear Barbie,
Today is Sunday Dec. 1. I'm not flying again today so I slept until 07:30 which is really kind of late for around here. I've been just sitting around doing nothing all day. I did get out a little and absorb some sun. It's kind of hot today about 85°.
I guess I got all my back mail last night. I got nine letters. A few were even from you. As for mailing yourself here I see no real big problem. You just get down to 5 lbs. and you can go airmail and be here in 4 days.

3 Dec. 68
Well your taxes just went up again yesterday.
I guess the Lord must have been watching over us because we crashed in our chopper. We weren't too far from the ground but all hell broke loose when we did hit. I was riding in front and my side hit the ground first and slid about 10 feet on its side until the rotor blades hit the ground and we then flipped about 7 times in every direction.
You see the rotor has 4 blades. 3 were tore off completely but the 4ᵗʰ one was about 4 ft. long and every time we hit ground it kept rotating and flipped the ship. All I remember is hitting the ground on my side and all the glass flying everywhere. After that I closed my eyes and just hung on. The motor flew out and scraped a little skin off of the gunner. Nothing too serious. I had to get x-rays on my arm but it's OK.

There was just nothing left of it so they burned it (the chopper) right there. It was only worth about 50 thousand so your taxes shouldn't go up too much.

I was real stiff this morning when I got up (at 8:30) so I didn't do much all day. I'm going to fly tomorrow again. As of right now I have the nickname of Crash.

Mom sent me a watch and a few goodies. She sent me some Koolaid so I mixed up about 2 gallons for everyone. It was real hot today.

Oh ya as for the $100 make good use of it. It doesn't look like I'll have much use for it.

I've got some more Christmas cards so if you can send me all the names and addresses of your relation I'll send them cards also.

And for the diamond bit you might just talk me into extending over here.

Tomorrow I'm flying as a gunner again. Well guess I'll hit the hay.
Love, *Sgt. Crash Heckman*

* * *

The vegetation in all directions was beaten down on the 40-year-old photo taken in Vietnam. Trees and shrubs were shattered from the force of the collision of chopper to earth, the ground black with fuel, mud, blood and debris, the scene spattered with silver shards of shattered glass. In the center of the crash site, rested what was left of an H13 Loach, Lee's observation chopper, called from hot spot to hot spot.

"As air reconnaissance, we seldom landed. We flew around and reported what we'd seen," Lee said. "We never went out without a Cobra flying above."

But they landed that day—crash landed.

As Lee described in his letter home, the men on board the Loach closed their eyes and hung on for their lives as they began their rapid descent. Overhead, men in the Cobra watched as Lee's chopper crashed and flipped—over and over and over.

"You were sure having fun," Lee was told later by one of the men aboard the Cobra. "You flopped seven times."

I guess the Lord must have been watching over us because we crashed in our chopper, Lee's letter began. By the time it was over, three blades were torn from the ship. The remaining blade kept rotating, causing the machine to continue to flip as well, as the motor flew out of the machine and shattered glass covered its occupants, like dirt scattered on a coffin.

Nothing too serious, Lee wrote.

Because helicopters were relatively slow, lightly armored and fragile, they were vulnerable to light arms fire from the enemy below. The nature of their operations required them to fly low, sometimes called up to land in enemy-controlled territory to deliver troops or supplies.

Consequently, in a ten-year time span from 1961 to 1971, the United States forces lost more than 2,000 helicopters to enemy action, and another 2,500+ to operational accidents, mishaps and weather. More than 22,000 helicopters were hit, many of them more than once.

"But when you write home to tell your mother, you make it sound like just a scratch," Lee said.

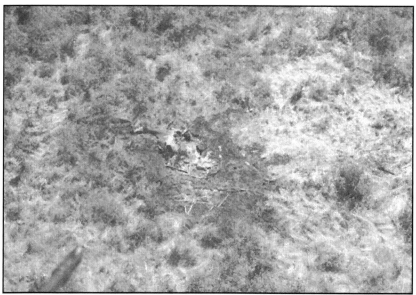

Remains of the Loach at the crash site

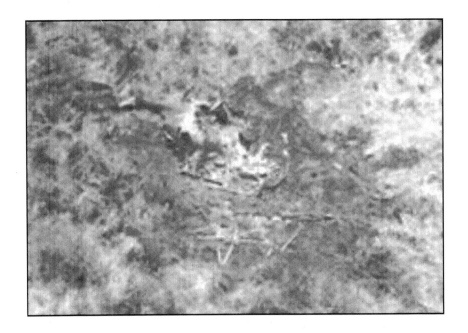

35

Sgt. Lee Heckman
December 2, 1968

Dear Barb,

Well I must explain that I am nearly drunk out of my mind but feel that I must write. I'm afraid my mom might get the news so I'll tell you to explain to her if she calls. If she doesn't forget it.

Today was a real disaster for us. We had 2 ships shot down and 4 shot up bad.

Anyhow 3 of our guys got killed and 6 wounded pretty bad. I got a small scratch on my wrist. So I imagine I'll get put in for a purple heart award. I'm just fine but mad because the round screwed up my M-60. So don't worry and I'm just fine.

Love
12/2/69

* * *

Lee's letters describe it in a few words—a day in the life of a Vietnam vet. Call it apprehension or horror, dread or panic, fear was a commodity in great supply among soldiers in Vietnam. Mental escape from the thought of future stressful combat situations could be found through self-medication. The route to escape for many was alcohol, and for others the drug of choice was marijuana, available at relatively low cost from Vietnamese civilians.

By the early 1970s, the Army attempted to crack down on marijuana use, but due to its prevalent nature the efforts were futile.

Soldiers, however, policed the use of marijuana themselves, largely restricting its use to base camps and other relatively secure installations.

The reasoning was simple: drug use in the field endangered lives. Even so, soldiers searched for escape in whatever means they could find.

Religion was never brought up in Vietnam, Lee Heckman said. One guy out of 100 wanted to go to church, in spite of their fear, anger or depression.

"When you're in the military and you experience symptoms of depression, you don't mention it. You were considered a weenie or wimpy, and there's not a chance of promotion. The Army says, 'If you don't feel good at what you're doing, kill a bunch more and you'll feel better.'"

Consequently, Lee blocked it all out. Blocked out the hell in which he was living. Blocked out dying. The only contact he had with a chaplain was when he was sent home, he said. Instead, he handled the stress and death that accompanied life in Vietnam with beer. Others turned to drugs, something of which Lee did not partake.

"I'm not saying alcohol was the right treatment," Heckman said, talking about the self-administered therapy available to soldiers stationed at the warfront. "That and the drugs that were smoked to cool their jets. Religion should have been, but alcohol seems to have been the treatment of choice for many."

Lee's letters tell of beer-drinking antics as could be expected from any typical young red-blooded male: buying cases of beer, stealing a refrigerator to store it in; and a drill sergeant selling answers to 40-question tests in exchange for money to buy a fifth of gin.

"Booze was part of our medication. We were just kids and we were getting our ass shot off every day. A tape player was one of the big things of that time, which shows you—we were just kids," Lee said.

Along with the coping mechanisms of beer and drugs, some men coped through escape—retreating into themselves.

36

Dear Barb,

Well I'm sorry if I have given you the wrong impression of how good it is here. There is some of the bad things: no transportation, our flight line is about 2 ½ blocks from our tent, P.X. is about 6 blocks away with nothing in it, cold outdoor showers which you take in the dark. It's about ½ block away and by the time you walk back through the dust you're just as dirty as before. Dust is real bad like every night you have to shake about ½ inch of dust off your bed.

We can't get any cleaning solvent for our weapons so we have to use diesel fuel. Many times we can't get new parts for our M60s so we have to use old parts. Food hasn't been too good lately so I guess I'll go on a diet like you said you were going to.

Yesterday I flew only one mission from 3:30-6:30. It was a real hot one. They had spotted a couple of companies of VC so they called in air strikes, etc. We were there and watched it. 2 jets dropped about a dozen 750 lb. bombs in the area plus all their rockets. They killed 78 and the rest moved west in a rubber tree plantation. They couldn't find exactly where they were so that was our job.

We flew over the area for about 2 hours trying to get them to shoot at us but they never did. I slept all morning. I now make up the schedule as to who flies the next day so I thought I'd take the day off. I think I'll go over to the P.X. later. I didn't get up until 8:30 a.m.

Like I told you we have about a dozen women around all the time for details such as raking the yard, taking out the evening trash, sweeping our floors, etc. Anyhow last week our 1ˢᵗ sergeant caught one of our guys in his area with one, kind of like going to it so now us NCOs have to watch them a little closer.

They only charge $5.00. That's sure cheaper than $22.50 huh.

Oh did I tell you all around here is a rubber plantation. There are trees for miles and miles.

I really don't know if you're interested in the ad I sent you but those are the type of choppers we fly.

Did I tell you our platoon sergeant got shot down the other day? He got shrapnel in his leg and is getting a purple heart. It's really only a small cut but they give awards away like mad.

We have some guys leaving us (men who were hurt were just gone with no reports given to soldiers back in base of their whereabouts) so we only have 14 men in our platoon now so the poor PVTs, PFC and Spec. 4s have K.P. and guard about every other night now. Too bad, huh?

I'm not sure if I can get any more pictures so you can maybe show these to my mother if you want to.

Also last week Charlie dropped 27 rounds of mortar on us. Sirens went off and everything but we all slept right through it.

Boy I sure hope I get my radio pretty soon.

As for your short dress maybe if you wash it a dozen times or so more it will shrink and be alright to wear when you pick me up at the airport when I come home. Please send any comments.

Well be good.

Love, Sgt. Lee

* * *

Lurch was his nickname. He was on his third tour in Vietnam.

"He just wanted to kill," Lee said. "He was a career killer. He was gonna die there. It was inevitable."

Lurch could open cans of beer with his teeth. He would shake a beer, poke out the bottom, and down the beer in 30 seconds. It was fascinating, Lee said. He met Lurch one night in Vietnam. The next day Lurch was dead. He was a door gunner.

"You didn't get close to people," Lee said, because the next day they could be gone. "Whatever we got into, we left, drank beer and partied." Fortunately for them, their job did not involve retrieving the dead like some of their fellow soldiers.

Lee and some of his fellow crew members felt they had ESP (extra sensory perception) about death.

"Quite often we would feel someone was going to die that day and we were right," Lee said. "So we never said that to anyone."

If Lee or a fellow crew member was supposed to fly that day and felt someone would die, they bailed out if they could. Because someone usually died, Lee said, when the premonitions hit. He didn't know what would have happened if they had mentioned their premonitions out loud. But, after the fact—and a few beers—they would talk about it.

"It was an eerie feeling. Not 100 percent fool proof but usually correct. But people would usually take a flight for you if you didn't want to fly that day. We were gung-ho kids. It was common to have hangovers, so it wasn't unusual to request that someone take a flight for you instead of admitting that you had a premonition."

Premonitions were plentiful in Vietnam, and after Lee returned home he had similar feelings—but only one time. When he got up that morning he knew someone would die that day. Sure enough, he said, shortly after he experienced the premonition he received notice that a coworker battling leukemia had died.

However scarce they were in the States, premonitions came naturally at a time and place when death surrounded soldiers stationed in Vietnam.

37

Dear Barb,

Well I made it back from R & R in real good shape. So now I'm all recovered and back for more action. My old Platoon Sergeant said he thinks I gained some weight. I had a pretty good time.

Today is the 4th and I'm back to flying. It's about noon and I only flew 1 hr. this morning.

As for the nasty pictures I sent a quite a few to Vic so you can contact him. I also sent him some pictures of some bad guys which I doubt you really want to see. If you call or see Vic tell him the background on the pictures is sand and not snow. OK.

Sorry I can't always think of romantic things to talk about but war is really hell. Even at night I try to think of things back in the world and you and the next thing I know I'm thinking about what I did that day and what I'll be doing the next day. This is really a full time job and it's just about all you think about. Guess this place gets to you after a while. Anymore I just can't wait until night and hope I get some letters so I can hear some news about back in the world even if it isn't really important. So you see your letters are very much appreciated.

As for the large envelope you got please tell me if you got everything in it I sent. People are known to take stuff like that, erase the name and put theirs in its place. Were the orders in it also?

I've got two more awards on the way. I don't know what one is but it will be pretty high because my pilot already got a silver star for the action and I was with him. Boy I'm getting tired of this here stuff. You get too many close calls for what you get out of it. I'm only going to fly 2 more months. I've already got over two rows of ribbons and that's enough.

Can you check how much Polaroid film costs for my camera. Don't buy any I just want to know the prices. OK.

Oh ya for those interested I got hit in the <u>right</u> wrist not the left. I'll have to be sure and show you my battle scars when I get back being it's on my wrist. Ha. Ha.

As for you going ahead and getting the papers for J.C. (Junior College), don't. I'll let you know which and what papers I need when I need them OK.

I've had a cold for about 2 weeks now and can't get rid of it. It all started when I got drunk and passed out on my bunk and didn't wake up when it got cold to cover myself. Well that's life.

Guess I better write my mother also.

Be good. Love, Lee

* * *

Telegram to Leon and Leona Heckman following one of several events of hostile action – From the Adjutant General

February 16, 1969
THE SECRETARY OF THE ARMY HAS ASKED ME TO INFORM YOU THAT YOUR SON SERGEANT LEE A HECKMAN WAS SLIGHTLY WOUNDED IN VIETNAM ON 12 FEB 69 AS A RESULT OF HOSTILE ACTION HE RECEIVED ABRASIONS AND GUNSHOT WOUND TO THE LEFT ARM WHILE PASSENGER ON A MILITARY AIRCRAFT ON COMBAT OPERATION WHEN AIRCRAFT WAS HIT BY HOSTILE SMALL ARMS FIRE. AIRCRAFT DID NOT CRASH OR BURN.

HE WAS TREATED AND (HOSPITALIZED IN VIETNAM) ADDRESS MAIL TO HIM AT THE HOSPITAL MAIL SECTION APO SF 96381. SINCE HE IS NOT REPEAT NOT SERIOUSLY WOUNDED NO FURTHER REPORTS WILL BE FURNISHED.

It could be as swift as a gunshot to the head; as simple as one step on a land mine. Now you see your buddy; now you don't.

"We are so blessed in the United States; everything here is nice. Secure. Safe," Lee said years later from the safety of his Nebraska home. "I can't explain it well enough. It's weird not to have a place to hide. In the United States, if your husband wales on you, you call 911, and the police come and help. You can run to the neighbors. If there's a tornado you can hide in the basement or in a culvert till it passes," Lee said. "But in Vietnam, where do you hide? When you're in Vietnam, you can't go AWOL. You can't hide in the culvert. There's *no* safe place. You go to bed and there are air strikes. Do you hide under your pillow or under your bed? In Vietnam, there were no guarantees. There was no safe place."

You think you'll get used to it after a time, Lee said, but that was never the case. "It's a very eerie feeling, not to be safe. The only thing you can do is to wait until your year is up."

But until then, men got a little jumpy, Lee said, explaining the need for R & R, a time of rest and recuperation, or rest and relaxation.

Soldiers were entitled to one or two inland R & R's and one big R & R within their tour of duty. Some visited Hawaii, for instance, for their big R & R. Lee took his inland R & R in Saigon. You could find anything you wanted in Saigon, Lee said. "Little kids would polish your boots as you walked down the street. They wanted a quarter."

They swarmed around soldiers' legs like hungry barn cats on the farm.

"We wouldn't have minded giving them a quarter but you never knew or not if they had a hand grenade. The Viet Cong would sacrifice a kid," Lee said. "They were not valuable."

The youngsters sold more than a boot shine. "The same kid would say, 'GI, I have a virgin sister. Five dollars.'"

Lee's impressions of Saigon are captured in black and white photographs: the buildings, Vietnamese women, the beach where a band played music. The musicians couldn't speak English, Lee said, but they sang American songs.

Horse and buggy took people from here to there and golfcart-type trolleys pulled visitors around. French buildings and large hotels were fronted with bombed craters, where mortar rounds had dug giant holes in the lawns.

Lee was starved for good things and took in the sights. He sampled French fries in Saigon.

"They were the best French fries I ever had in my life. Turns out they were turnips."

38

Dear Barb,

Well I'm laying here in bed listening to some good music. You see I broke down and bought myself a Christmas present. I got a "national" tape recorder. So now maybe I can talk you into buying me some tapes. Maybe you can tape some of your records also. (Only Golden Oldies please)

I'm pretty sure all tapes are the same but I'll give you a little information about it anyway. It will play tape speeds at 1 7/8, 3 ¾ or 7 ½. 3 ¾ is the best tape speed for the temperature over here. It will play up to a 7-inch reel. The voltage is adjustable from 80-250 amps. It has dual built in speakers. If you send any don't send just too many because we do move around and can't have too much stuff.

We didn't move yet but will any day. Guess we're going someplace near Long Bihn.

I have been flying every day for about 2 weeks now. We don't put in that many hours but you sure get tired. We have been going into an area where there hasn't been any GI's for over 2 years so we are finding and getting into all sorts of stuff. Today we were in a free fire zone and saw a suspicious looking bunch of trees so I opened up with my M-60 and put about 100 rounds right through a platoon of our own men (through the thick trees, not knowing). I don't think we hit anyone but we all got a scare and they found out they were in the wrong area.

Back again

Oh ya on the tapes other speeds are OK and 2 track tapes only. It will play 4 track though but 2 track is better.

I had the day off today. I sure was in a bad mood. You see there is no

Christmas spirit around here and on Christmas everyone just kind of feels sorry for themselves.

I had a little trouble with a Spec. 5 trying to tell me what to do the other day. A Spec. 5 is specialized in a certain job and I'm a noncommissioned officer so I do outrank him. I had the pleasure of informing him that. Our Platoon Sergeant heard about it later and chewed him out again for trying to talk to me the way he did. He was clearly put out that us NCO's run the platoon.

We found an elephant the other day. We were going to kill it but it was too late in the day.

We flew down a river (Som Bae) and found a raft with a pack and A.K. (enemy) rifle on it tied to the bank. We wanted to go down and get the rifle as a war trophy but thought it might be an ambush or booby trap so I just shot it up. I shot about a thousand rounds in the area and even shot a tree down beside it so I know no one will ever use that weapon. It's fun to fly down rivers. We fly about one or two feet above the water and the banks and trees are high above us on our sides. We usually go from 20-80 m.p.h. down there because it's kind of dangerous.

Yesterday we were in an area where they knew there were a thousand Charlies there but it was a 3 layer canopy. We flew over the area for two hours but they wouldn't shoot at us so we could pinpoint them.

We also got 6 thousand Charlies in the area around here so things are pretty hot. We have been having extra guard at night because they thought we were going to get overrun.

Our team just got beat at volleyball. We won one and lost one.

Got your large card tonight. Everyone was mad because they didn't get any mail. They said mine took all the room.

Well I've got 1ˢᵗ flight tomorrow and have to get up at 5:30 to get everyone else up.

So, With love, Lee

* * *

It was the job of Air Reconnaissance to report places the Viet Cong had broken into. If they saw anything suspicious—dog tracks, humans, bicycles, anything besides jungle—they reported it.

One day, Lee's Loach flew over an area that didn't look quite right. The region was a free fire zone and the pilot gave the order to fire. Lee carried out his orders. The trees were thick and impossible to see through, but the area looked suspicious and Lee did his job. He peppered the area with gunfire.

Forty years later, Lee recalls the horror of seeing American troops run out of the area.

"I like to think I didn't hurt anybody," he said.

But as he looks back, Lee ponders the truth of the day: if his machine gun was capable of firing 450-500 rounds a minute, and they blasted the area for 10 minutes, he'd have had to have killed somebody.

"I thought at the time nobody got hurt, but when you get to be my age you think about it...."

LaRayne M. Topp

39

Dear Barb,

I haven't flown for 5 days now. I was getting a little jumpy and my nerves needed the rest. Believe me this work gets the best of you.

I'm going to fly tomorrow. One of our choppers got shot up pretty bad today. The gunner had 3 bullets come up through the floor all around him but didn't get hit.

As for me to tell you stuff that really isn't too bad that kind of leaves out everything.

Dear Barb,

Did you hear about the 2/12 Cav getting wiped out. That was just north of here. It's now 2:30 and I just got back from another mission. We found where we got mortared from last night. We found the empty shells, trails and bunkers but no V.C.

Dear Barb,

I lucked out again the other day. We were flying right over an explosion when it went off. It threw some shrapnel through the engine compartment but didn't stop us. The impact threw us around a little in the air but everything turned out OK.

Dear Barb,

Oh ya that wasn't me in the newspaper ad you sent me. Actually it was worse because 70 out of the 90 were killed or taken prisoner. One medevac chopper was shot down killing all 12. But I guess that's war and you can expect that. I think you asked me if I knew where the other guys are that I came over with. Well I don't know where they are and don't know anything about them.

Dear Barb,

Thursday 3 people in A Troop crashed and burned to death and Friday 3 more people crashed and burned to death so we now have to always wear our fireproof flight suits.

Dear Barb,

Yesterday we flew into an ambush. They had 2, 30-caliber machine guns and about 15 AK rifles. They all opened up on us but we only got hit once in the tail rotor. Later on another one of our ships got shot at and the gunner got shot in the arm.

Dear Barb,

Just got back from helping another troop. Another one of their scout birds got shot down in the same place we have been having all the trouble.

Dear Barb,

You will never guess what I did in the line of work yesterday and today—Nothing.

The day before yesterday I flew 10 hours. I got in about 7:30 that night and there was no food left so I said the heck with it and went over to the officers and drank all their beer. Boy did we get into a conversation about life, why we're here, infinity, Mars, space, religion, twilight zone, etc. I made it to bed about 1 or 2. I slept all day yesterday in a sick stage.

Today I fixed a shelf for my tape recorder and speakers. I put a roof over my little apartment and put red paper over the light so it looks like you're going into a night club or something.

I finished the day by taping tapes.

As for your taping some records for me if you don't want to or aren't too interested and can't afford it just forget it. I guess I know other people that got some pretty good records also. Or if you need the money for the tapes I'll send it to you. Might as well let you put it to use since I'm not sure I'll make it out of here to spend it myself.

Today at 2,000 ft. one of our helicopter engines froze up and started on fire. The chopper is designed to auto rotate and it kind of floated into a real nice rice paddy with about 5 ft. of water but everyone made it out OK.

5 other of our ships have been shot down the last week and a half. They really don't play for games. Maybe you heard about all the weapons and ammo we captured.

I'm going to send you a couple of awards I got. When you get done doing whatever you want with them you can give them to my mother and she can put them with the rest of my stuff.

I'm sending you the picture of what was left of the chopper I crashed in. Please take real good care of it since it's the only one. Can you do your best to get some duplicates of it maybe even a little bigger. I know it's possible even if it is color.

I got a bunch of pictures here I'm sure would really turn you on or else make you mad. And your sex book only shows 10 ways. Ha!

Well be good.

Love, Lee

* * *

Lee's letters tell of several warrant officers who served as pilots for reconnaissance choppers. They were given the courtesy title of Mister instead of having their names preceded by their rank. Mr. James was often the pilot for the helicopters in which Lee flew.

Lee recalled some of the warrant officer's antics. "Mr. James could fly around, find a building, and then gently hook the skid of the chopper under a roof to gently pull it up and see what's there," Lee said.

On one memorable occasion, however, a 2nd Lieutenant served as the pilot. The officer had heard about Mr. James' abilities, so while searching out a particular building, he'd decided to lift the roof of it, just as he'd heard Mr. James could do. The pilot hooked onto the roof and attached the chopper's skids. The building—with 500 bushels of rice stored inside—held fast.

"Down we went," Lee said, and what began as a simple task soon became a complicated nightmare, as metal, glass and steel collided with the blood red soil of Vietnam. Lee Heckman recalled falling in slow motion, landing below in warm, murky water. The thick, yellow-green, razor-sharp elephant grass—with strands standing twice as tall as a Viet Cong—surrounded him in the water like enemy soldiers.

His breathing exploded in hard spasms as he huddled in the grass, shivering and praying that he would be saved by friendly forces before he was taken prisoner or executed by not-so-friendly Viet Cong.

The barrel of his M-16 packed with mud, he ordered his heart to quit pounding so loud, his heavy breathing to quiet. Surely the enemy would hear it and trace the sounds to him. Fear enveloped him.

He asked himself if the pilot and door gunner made it to safety or if he was the sole survivor. "In my mind, I asked myself, did they live or was I alone? I didn't realize it at the time but my rifle was plugged, should I have had to use it...."

In the air, his chopper flew next to God, Lee said, but lying there, hurting and bleeding in the elephant grass, he was at the mercy of the Viet Cong. Viet Cong bullets made quick work of foot soldiers; there was little room for American grunts in Vietnamese prisons.

But soldiers who fell from the sky might be pilots, and pilots might know something. Pilots were valuable, taken to prisons like the Hanoi Hilton, a notorious Viet Cong prison, and tortured for their secrets.

In a flash the grass parted, and Lee Heckman, terrified and alone, waited to be killed. But... it was the good guys helping me, he recalled.

"It would have been nice if they could have hollered to tell me they were coming. It could have prevented a near heart attack for me," he said. "I am very sure to this day that is why I don't like people coming up on me with no warning. I get very pissed, my blood pressure goes up and my mind flashes back to that day of being startled. It can take several days to get back to normal."

40

Well there ain't no time to wonder why,
Whoopee! we're all gonna die.
        "I Feel Like I'm Fixin' To Die" by Country Joe and the Fish

* * *

It was to be Lee's last venture into Vietnam fighting. A chopper had been shot down. Rescue calls went out, calling for reinforcements, ground troops, choppers, everyone and anyone in the area.

The three men in Lee's Loach responded. Below them, a chopper had crashed in a clearing, its passengers strewn about. In a building about 100 yards away, the enemy continued its relentless fire.

Ground troops ran rescue missions as they were able in Vietnam. They wrote reports, took down information and cleaned up downed planes. Those were not Lee's jobs.

"We didn't run the whole war ourselves," he said.

Even so, Lee and his crew were first on the scene.

"The men were laying there. How do I know from the air if they are alive or not? They're not moving," was how Lee described the scene. There was no way of telling how long ago the crash happened. Fifteen minutes? An hour?

Lee's boss, the pilot, landed the chopper between the crash site and the building, gunfire exploding from every window and doorway.

"Heckman, get out and go over there and help," the pilot barked.

Understandably, Lee didn't want to go, but he did not refuse.

"I was scared that day to see the tracer rounds coming at me, Lee said." But he followed orders as he thought to himself, "They're already dead, and if they're dead, they're dead. I didn't have an answer of how to help dead people."

Although he couldn't carry around extra ammo, and in spite of his reservations and his fears, Lee had one foot out the door. He was trained by the U.S. Army so that if and when the day arrived, instinct would take over.

"You just do what you're told to do," Lee said.

But the pilot quickly changed his mind. He decided to keep Lee, as door gunner, inside the chopper with a M-60 machine gun in hand, and instead sent out the observer with his M-16 rifle.

It was suicide.

"They plugged him right away," Lee said. "It was a waste of life."

Shots were coming at them from all directions, and as quickly as the pilot gave the observer the order to head out, he picked up the chopper, circling round and round in the air above the crash site. He gave Lee the command to fire.

The angle of the chopper was such that Lee couldn't see the ground below. Tracers from the building below whistled past them, ground into the chopper, shattered the glass. Lee was shooting randomly, wildly, into the air. The barrel of his M-60 was red hot. He was a kid; he was excited.

"I couldn't even see what I was firing at," he recalled years later. But he did what he was told. He made noise and kept firing to keep the enemies' heads down so that U.S. air forces—now surrounding Lee's chopper—might be able to rescue the soldiers below.

The live soldiers.

If there were any.

And then they got the hell out of there.

Years later, with a pile of letters from home along with his discharge papers, Lee looks back in retrospect.

"In the coulda, shoulda, I ask myself, 'Did I kill anyone?' I'm not saying I shot him, but if you aim and hit, you know for sure. I hope everything, every bullet, went where it was supposed to go, but I ask myself, now, 'Did I kill anyone?'"

Lee asks himself what he calls a *personal question*: "Why did we drop the observer off and then leave?"

He asks other questions: "What value would there be to remain there and get killed? With ground troops and Cobras coming in, as scouts we had no purpose there. What would we do there but get in the way?"

They are answers Lee will never have. After Lee's last attempt to save the lives of his fellow soldiers, Lee's Dad made his final attempt to save Lee's life. On March 6, 1969, Lee received word from home. His dad had died that morning.

And on March 6, 1969, Lee's letters home ended.

LaRayne M. Topp

41

There are three side effects of acid: enhanced long-term memory, decreased short-term memory, and I forget the third.
Timothy Leary

* * *

As soldiers fought and died in Vietnam, back home people also fought—and some died—protesting the war. Tension was especially visible among a culture—or counterculture—of people who followed the phrase coined by American psychologist Timothy Leary to "turn on, tune in, drop out." Known later in life for advocating research into psychedelic drugs for their therapeutic, emotional and spiritual benefits, Leary's influence was widely felt in the late 1960s and early 1970s by the Hippies.

With roots in the Beatnik and Bohemian traditions of earlier times, Hippies often expressed themselves in colorful ways: long hair and headbands; beaded necklaces and bracelets; tie-dyed t-shirts and velvet tunics; fringed jackets, heavy leather belts, embroidered blue jeans and bare feet.

Anti-war protests by the Hippies began as early as 1965, originating in California and gradually spreading across the United States. By the year 1968, when Lee Heckman was facing deployment to Vietnam, massive Hippie-led Peace Marches filled American city streets, along with student demonstrations at college and university campuses across the country.

Most Hippies ranged in age from 15 to 25, primarily from wealthy middle class families. Rejecting their parents' conservative ways of life, Hippies fought what they perceived as white man's perverted society of pollution, war and greed. Many of those attending colleges dropped out to embrace lifestyles that included more sexual freedom, less work and less ambition, coupled with drug-infused meditation.

Musical festivals clouded with the smoke of pot and blurred with LSD trips and beer binges attracted singers tuned in to guitars, banjos and drums, along with thousands of young people intent on making love, not war. They made their anti-war beliefs known through pacifist folk songs and peaceful sit-ins and human be-ins, along with not-so-peaceful protests and rallies.

For four days in August of 1969, while three people died from bad LSD trips and heroin overdoses at a rock concert held at a little known spot in New York known as Woodstock, on the other side of the world more than 100 American soldiers died while serving their country in Vietnam.

Hippies went so far as to protest the war by placing beautiful flowers into the gun barrels of National Guard Troops posted as a sentry at the nation's Pentagon, demonstrating a more peace-filled way to use weapons than a discharge of deadly bullets.

While Hippies were stuffing flowers into gun barrels, Lee Heckman was setting down his machine gun after the last fierce battle, trying to rescue men from a downed chopper. He was called into the office on base and the Captain gave him the news: Lee's father had died.

The Captain asked Lee if he wanted to go home.

Of course.

The captain told Lee that if he wanted to go home, the procedure had been changed and now Lee would have to go up country to Da Nang to get the proper paperwork. The Captain said he couldn't cut the orders at the base.

"You don't hop on a train or a bus in Vietnam," Lee said. "It would have taken a week to get across the country."

So Lee hooked up with a chaplain. The chaplain called someone, and *someone* said, "Nope, the Captain was correct. The Army had changed the policy."

But the chaplain was insistent. He called up the chain of command. Lee had heard that morning his father had died, and by 11:00 that night the chaplain informed Lee he'd be going home.

"They opened Finance to get money for me to go home. They opened the office and cut the orders that night," Lee said.

The next morning at daylight, the same captain who had refused Lee's request sat beside Lee in the captain's personal chopper, flying to Saigon. "I sure had some choice words for him," Lee recalled years later, but at the time he said nothing. "If it wouldn't have been for that chaplain I wouldn't have gotten to go home. I never thanked him. I wish I had."

The route home included a stop at Hawaii, before landing at Oakland, California. The runway for the Oakland airbase is situated on the ocean. "All I saw was water as the plane was going down. I knew we would land in the ocean," Lee said. "Before I heard the wheels hit the runway I thought we would drown. I hadn't come all this way to land in the ocean!"

As Lee made his way into the airport, a Hippie confronted him. His long hair and beaded tunic in direct contrast to Lee's closely cropped head and Army uniform, the Hippie waved an antiwar poster in the air as he aimed a stream of spit in Lee's war-weary face.

"You baby killer," the Hippie shouted. "You stinking baby killer."

"I was all hepped up, my dad had just died, and at the airport were hippies with posters. They hadn't participated in the war; they didn't work; they had time to hang around the airports and protest," Lee said.

Lee ends the story in few words. The Hippie spit in his face. The Hippie went home without his teeth. A policeman nearby watched the entire incident. He walked over to where Lee was. The two smiled at each other and without saying a word, both walked off in separate directions.

As Lee made his way back home to Nebraska, he knew he couldn't live a life packed with the kind of anger he'd just exploded with in the airport. He determined he would try to make a better lover than a fighter.

"I couldn't live my life that way. I couldn't hit people anymore."

Lee Heckman never again picked up a gun to take a life. Any life.

LaRayne M. Topp

42

Combat is fast, unfair, cruel, and dirty. It is meant to be that way so that the terrible experience is branded into the memory of those who are fortunate enough to survive. It is up to those survivors to ensure that the experience is recorded and passed along to those who just might want to try it.
"Force Recon Diary, 1969: The Riveting, True-to-Life Account of Survival and Death in One of the Most Highly Skilled Units in Vietnam"
by Bruce H. Norton

* * *

Lee made 4 ½ months of his tour of duty in Vietnam and was coming on strong when he was called home because his father died. He speculates the letters his aunt, sisters and other family members sent to Nebraska's legislators, congressmen and senators, saying Lee was his mother's sole surviving son, resulted in orders placing him stateside.

He received the letter containing his orders while still on funeral leave at his mother's home at Norfolk, Nebraska. With only five or six months of his enlistment remaining, and high hopes that he wouldn't feel like a draft dodger, Lee made his way to his new station at Fort Riley, Kansas.

As he arrived, his commanding officer asked, "How would you like to work in the office right here?"

Lee could hardly believe his good fortune. "I didn't do a thing," Lee said of his months there. "The whole office was filled with soldiers with problem histories. The Sergeant had a feeling for people who'd gotten banged up."

Lee made his way to Nebraska every weekend to see Barb, his girlfriend. A fellow soldier routinely rode along back home with him.

While stationed at Ft. Riley, Lee retrieved a soldier who had gone AWOL in Kentucky. Lee had completed A.I.T. training in Kentucky so he was anxious to see the base once again.

But when he arrived at the Kentucky base, little was familiar. "There was not a person there I knew," Lee said. "It was a lonely feeling."

The soldier Lee was sent to retrieve was just a little kid who went AWOL, Lee said, but he was "kind of cocky. He became a little intimidated, however, by Lee with all the medals on his chest, especially when Lee took out his 45 pistol and told the young man he knew how to use it.

"I had absolutely no trouble with him after that," Lee recalled.

43

You wouldn't know the platoon any more. All new dudes. There isn't anyone left except me, Forten and Chorncet.
                              Letter from Lee's former platoon sergeant

* * *

They used to call it shell-shock. You saw World War II veterans suffering from the condition in the nursing home. Now they call it posttraumatic stress disorder, more familiarly known to Lee Heckman as PTSD.

He is familiar enough with the condition to describe it distinctly. In a typical life a person can easily recall one life-changing experience, he said, or maybe two. A car wreck. A house fire. The loss of a spouse or child. The memory of it is that person's one bad experience.

For Lee, a multitude of things made up his bad experiences, all taking place on the battlefield of Vietnam. He can't say which one was the worst one, which near-death experience put him over the edge. Was it living in a war zone or the constant machine gun fire? Seeing your buddies get hit? Enemy bullets and schrapnel zeroing in on you from every angle? Torn limbs? Disfigurement? Death?

"Heckling from Hippies didn't bring about PTSD; near death did it," he said.

Posttraumatic stress disorder can affect a person immediately after a major trauma or it can come to visit months later. It can last for several months, a number of years, or a lifetime. PTSD may be prompted by a natural disaster such as a flood or fire, or life-impacting events such as war, terrorist attacks, assault, domestic abuse or rape.

People plagued with PTSD re-experience the event with mental, emotional and sometimes physical reactions. They can feel as if they are actually experiencing the event one more terrifying time. In other words, the memories get frozen in time, as the pain, hurt and sorrow of past events reignite the present tense. The very memories of the experiences that kept a soldier alive, might be the stumbling block upon the return stateside.

A simple trip to the grocery store or a crowded wedding reception might be a place of unease. A box in the middle of the highway might contain a bomb. There's even the danger of being alone.

PTSD victims cope with these experiences in a number of ways. They may become emotionally numb or live their lives in a daze of detachment. They may be unable to recall the details of the event prompting their PTSD, have difficulty concentrating on routine tasks, become irritable or angry, or have difficulty sleeping. Others avoid people or places that remind them of the triggering event, and still others live life in dread, with a sense of having no future.

Survivor's guilt is often coupled with PTSD. Those who survived the war feel they must have done something wrong to have survived when others did not. Survivor's guilt is a significant symptom of PTSD, and rears its ugly head in the reactions of anxiety, depression, social withdrawal, physical complaints, sleep disturbance and nightmares.

In May of 1969, Lee received a letter from a platoon sergeant, telling him of the death of all but two soldiers in Lee's platoon, including Mr. James, the warrant officer who served as pilot for the chopper in which Lee flew.

You wouldn't know the platoon any more. All new dudes. There isn't anyone left except me, Forten and Chorncet, the soldier wrote. Four of Lee's fellow soldiers were killed in action within two weeks of each other.

Perhaps that's what contributed to his decision upon his discharge to direct his mother to burn his uniform and any paperwork or medals associated with it. The PTSD cocktail Lee's forced to down each day comes complete with a survivor's guilt chaser. It's blended with nightmares of drowning, anything and everything, he said.

"I remember lots of things. These lots of things turn into a blur. In the middle of night, I'm kicking and screaming, and I'm right there."

Lee often awakens screaming and sweating, so instead of enduring that nightmare of a wake-up call, he has programmed himself not to sleep. He roams the house at night instead.

"It's easier to sleep in the daytime, and if I'm in a secure place, I sleep better."

He avoids crowds. If he can't avoid them, he doesn't stay long. When he goes out in public, he sits with his back to the wall. Loud noises disturb him. People coming up behind him can drive him into a flash back, back into the elephant grass, waiting for death.

"It's the flashbacks, the bullets," Lee said.

When he gets startled, he's not startled for only a second but for several weeks. "I see someone coming at me with a rifle or a knife. I don't get over it right away. I'm riled for a week or two. I'm pissy to the whole world. It's hard for people to understand that."

From what Lee has read about PTSD, it doesn't get better; it gets worse. According to some statistics, one out of six Vietnam Vets are affected by PTSD.

"How you're put together mentally decides who will be affected with PTSD and who won't," Lee explained. "And what your job was— if you were a in a non-combat job and never saw action, or falling out of helicopters and getting shot at."

"During combat, you kept your distance. You never got close to anyone," Lee said about ways to cope in Vietnam. A man who could be your best buddy one night could be dead the next day. "People die. Get transferred. You were devastated if you were close to someone and they were dead."

Plus, and even more real, you could be dead yourself by morning.

It follows through in life, Lee maintains. If you call getting close to someone a defect, Lee explained, that too is a spinoff of PTSD.

"When it's all done they say to live with it. Ironically, the only way to prevent a tragic problem is not to have the tragic problem happen," Lee said of PTSD treatment. "You learn to live with it."

Many veterans of Nam suffer from sleep disorders, depression, alcoholism, suicide, or distancing from family and friends, Lee said. They build walls. The ways that posttraumatic stress disorder plays out haunts them.

Lee's experiences in Vietnam affected his marriage, which ended in divorce. He thinks he was a good father, but could have had a closer relationship with his two sons and daughter if it weren't for Nam, he said. He is at high risk for suicide. He was encouraged by a veterans' officer to apply for disability. As a result of filling out paperwork to receive compensation for disability, Lee finally received a number of the medals he was due for his service in Vietnam.

While on active duty with the U.S. Army, I served as an observer and door gunner aboard H-13 Loach while in the Republic of VietNam. At no time did I have anything for exposure to loud noises. There was continual noise from the aircraft and from the M-60 machine gun. Some days, I would expend upwards to 10,000 rounds. On three or four times I went down with the aircraft. Pictures of crash site included along with photos of deceased. Death was all around us. Flying reconnaissance missions, we were exposed to death and destruction most every time we went out. I started having re-occuring nightmares shortly after my arrival in the country. It is something I lived with. I have difficulty sleeping, I basically toss and turn most of the night and wake up tired. The nightmares just don't go away. I received a purple heart and Army Commendation Medal with "V" device for my service.

One thing led to another in the application process, and the next thing Lee knew he was talking to a shrink. The doctor, familiar with PTSD, said historically the number one cause of posttraumatic stress syndrome was and is being a gunner.

The doctor asked Lee what *one* thing brings about flashbacks.

Lee's response: What *one* thing? How can you choose *one* thing when you were facing your own death every day?

The shrink asked him about his hobbies.

Lee's response? Work and drinking beer.

In fact, throwing himself into his work upon his return to the states was Lee's coping mechanism to the memories of Vietnam.

44

Walking through this park-like area, the memorial appears as a rift in the earth—a long, polished black stone wall, emerging from and receding into the earth. Approaching the memorial, the ground slopes gently downward, and the low walls emerging on either side, growing out of the earth, extend and converge at a point below and ahead. Walking into the grassy site contained by the walls of this memorial, we can barely make out the carved names upon the memorial's walls. These names, seemingly infinite in number, convey the sense of overwhelming numbers, while unifying these individuals into a whole..."

From Maya Ying Lin's winning competition entry for Vietnam Veterans Memorial, 1981

* * *

"We were kids. It was exciting." That's how Lee Heckman describes his feelings when he was sent to Vietnam.

At first.

It wasn't until he got home that he became angry. He had been injured and lived with the effects of his collective experiences. His dad died while he was gone. He had lived in a land where there was no place to hide from the stray bullet or the well-aimed bomb. He was sick, coughing and coughing, for a year. He was experiencing the symptoms of posttraumatic stress disorder.

The Hippie who met him at the airport may have been speaking for the many in the country for which Lee fought, spitting out the derisive name of *baby killer.*

"The whole country was against us. People who sent us stabbed us in the back. It's a democratic country and the country voted. We agreed to go. We didn't ask to come home and be called names.

So Lee handled it by not handling it, by not bringing it up.

"We didn't say anything about being in the service once we got home." After all, they'd lost the war.

Lee married the woman he'd written to for two years, and they bought a drive-in, the Dog and Suds. He ran a car body shop at the same time. He and his wife raised three kids. He wanted to be busy. He didn't want to have time to think. He didn't want his mind to idle.

"I didn't want to think about crap," he said.

But sometimes he would begin to talk about his experiences in Vietnam, to explain what his time in hell was like, to tell his close friends, his wife, his children. Invariably, the listeners would change the subject to the weather.

He mentioned to a neighbor that a gunner's time spent in Nam was measured in one of two ways: You flew six months or recorded 100 confirmed kills.

Lee was asked what a confirmed kill was.

Lee said, "Have you seen a deer hit on the highway?"

His neighbor said, "Oh, why'd you tell me that? That sounds awful!"

And changed the subject.

This scenario was repeated across the United States, surrounding the veterans of Vietnam. As the years went by, people from the United States came to realize that Vietnam Veterans had been treated unfairly, poorly, downright wretchedly on their return home. With Vietnam as a learning experience, during later wars yellow ribbons were hung on trees, stories were written, and television and radio interviews told of the valiant fighting, the patriotism of soldiers headed to wars overseas.

Lee and fellow Vietnam veterans remember the welcome home from Vietnam they never received.

"I'm probably jealous," Lee said. "The only welcome home from Vietnam went to draft dodgers who came home from Canada."

Consequently, instead of talking about Vietnam, Lee has avoided the subject entirely. But that's not all he avoids. He avoids the reminders.

The pop-pop-pop of helicopters or fireworks sounding like the gunfire of Vietnam and will send him under the table or out the door. The vantage point gives him a chance to see where the sound is coming from, and as he says, "Even with 40 years of dealing with posttraumatic stress disorder, it makes you jumpy."

He avoids guns; he doesn't go hunting.

One day his youngest son asked him to sight a new gun he had purchased, setting up tin cans in a row across the yard. Instead of aiming, Lee shot the gun from the hip. A direct hit.

"Lucky shot," his son said.

So Lee did it again.

A second son—watching—was impressed.

On another occasion, his daughter as a grade schooler, watched a nightly television news about guerilla warfare. She turned to her dad and said, "Dad they're fighting gorillas!"

He smiled to himself, but didn't explain further.

When the bloodmobile comes to town, Lee avoids it. His reasoning relates to Vietnam.

"If a soldier gave blood there was no physical training for him that day, so we all gave blood. Try to do pushups when you're a quart low."

He has never registered to vote.

"I wanted to vote at the time I went to Nam but I wasn't old enough. I was not old enough to drink, but I was old enough to go to Vietnam. What's more important than that but I wasn't able to vote.

"I'm an old German," he explained. "When I get pissed, I'm pissed. I'll put up with a lot but when it gets up to here..." He levels his hand at his chin, and leaves the sentence unfinished.

Sometimes he watches documentaries about the Vietnam War. He nods when he hears a comment from a veteran of the U.S. Civil War: "A bunch of us went to Gettysburg. Some of us didn't come home. And if you weren't there you won't ever understand."

Lee's niece—his goddaughter—and her husband adopted a son from Vietnam. He met the little boy on the day of his baptism.

"It was kind of tough," Lee says of the experience.

"He wants to kiss you," the baby's new parents said.

Lee had an upset stomach after the baptism. He didn't go to the house for the reception.

He avoids other things, like vaccinations. He took enough for a lifetime when heading to Vietnam. He keeps no pills or drugs in the house beyond a cough drop or two. In fact, he bought a box of cherry cough drops twenty years ago; they're still in his medicine cabinet, unopened. He made a decision while in Vietnam not to do drugs, although he admits with a grin that there is usually a Coors Light in the frig, his old standby painkiller.

To this day, Lee does his best to stay away from mortuary visitations or funerals.

And finally, he avoids the Vietnam Memorial.

Lee traveled with his family to Washington D.C. They were intent on visiting the glistening black wall of the Vietnam Memorial, chiseled with more than 50,000 names of Vietnam veterans who met their maker in Vietnam.

"I stayed on the sidelines," Lee said. "It was just like going to the mortuary."

Epilogue

"There's many a boy here today that looks upon war as all glory, but boys, it is all hell!"
   William T. Sherman, General of the Union Army during the American Civil War

* * *

And so ends one man's lifelong, backward look at Vietnam. More than forty years since the war has ended, its repercussions are still being felt, the shock waves of gun shots reverberating through the stillness of life. Some Vietnam veterans have managed to put the war far, far behind them, refusing to take in the scene from that rear view mirror.

Others nurse physical problems: cracked skulls and bad backs caused by chopper crashes, shattered arm and leg bones fragmented by bullets and mortar shells, skin and tissue imbedded with shrapnel—all reminders of a war long past. Some of them struggle with the mental and emotional aftereffects of war: posttraumatic stress disorder, alcoholism or depression. Others deal with the possible consequences of Agent Orange: Parkinson's disease, heart disease and diabetes.

Few of them returned home from war to the victory celebrations experienced by veterans of World War II, or the yellow ribbon-wrapped trees greeting returnees from Grenada, the Persian Gulf War, Kuwait, and Operation Iraqi Freedom. Vietnam veterans, such as Lee Heckman, never felt the appreciation from American citizens as did those fighting at Operations across the sea: Operation Desert Storm,

Operation Desert Shield and Operation Desert Fox; or those battling the War on Terrorism in Iran or Afghanistan.

Instead, upon their return to the United States, numerous Vietnam veterans were spit upon and reviled with defamatory labels, cruel and offensive. In some cases, they weren't welcomed into the very organizations dedicated to making life easier for veterans of earlier wars.

Lee Heckman is one of the Vietnam veterans who's had time to digest what the war meant to him. When he sees young men and women who are heading off to wartime missions today, he knows they, like Lee at that formative stage in his life, are idealistic about the job they're being asked to do. They believe they're doing the right thing.

So did Lee.

Lee Heckman, like countless others before him and others still to come, picked up their rifles, took control of a tank or chopper, naval ship or submarine, as those in command made crystal clear which way, how long and how much. Trapped in the moment and a survival mode, soldiers have been caught up in the task before them.

It's why the Army preys on the young, Lee says. "It's why the Army doesn't send old people off to battle. The old would say 'This is stupid,' and not follow orders."

"The Army brainwashes you," Lee says. "It has to. Soldiers can't be involved in war without their heart and soul in it. They trick you into killing. You get caught up in it. You do your job."

So did Lee.

He just didn't know that the fallout from this job would end up being an uninvited and unwelcome guest at every holiday gathering, family event, work schedule or leisure time activity from his release from active duty throughout eternity.

And speaking of eternity...

Lee's beliefs are impacted by his faith. He's a believer in Christ's message of peace.

"I was brought up in the church, hearing and believing 'Thou shalt not kill.' But you're trained to defend yourself."

However, now that Lee's had some time to ponder this training, he has come to question the kind of wartime duty a government asks of its citizenry.

And it isn't just the Vietnam War Lee believes the United States shouldn't have become involved in, but the majority of them.

"We've never won a war really," he says. "We might think we won World War II, but they outgunned us later on with their technology. We went to war because we were afraid of Communism. But is that so bad? Some people need a dictator; they can't function on their own. It's terrorists now, not communists, who send us to war."

Lee continues: "In Korea we lost a lot of lives and may have prevented their Civil War. In the Gulf War, we only gained an airbase. We say we won in Iraq, but we still have people there."

And as for Vietnam, Lee is firm: "We had bogus information back then to go over there in the first place, but we were too proud to back out."

Some of that information was provided by Robert McNamara who served as the U.S. Secretary of Defense from 1961 through 1968. Although McNamara played a large role in escalating the United States' involvement in the Vietnam War, years later he mourned those decisions.

In the book, *The Fog of War* by James G. Blight and Janet M. Lang, Robert McNamara is quoted as saying the United States was the strongest nation in the world, fighting the Vietnam War unsupported by allies.

"Not Japan, not Germany, not Britain or France. If we can't persuade nations with comparable values of the merit of our cause, we'd better re-examine our reasoning." He closed with this comment: "War is so complex it's beyond the ability of the human mind to comprehend. Our judgment, our understanding, are not adequate. And

Memorial Boot Ceremony for the dead

we kill people unnecessarily."

Lee's thoughts exactly.

As Lee looks back, he sees Vietnam as a political war, guided by the politicians instead of the military. When U.S. troops were strategizing to take out major bridges, railroads or freight lines, they had to back out so as not to offend Russia or Red China, Lee says.

"The war was a poorly run show."

Perhaps it would have been better for all concerned if U.S. troops hadn't shown up for the war games at all. No doubt about it: the United States would have lost fewer soldiers if it would have kept its troops at home, if the draft boards hadn't selected each losing card from the deck of recruitment possibilities, if the United States had folded before it ever asked to lay any chips on the table in Vietnam.

The way Lee sees it, both the North and the South sides of the Vietnamese Demilitarized Zone may have lost fewer soldiers and civilians if they'd have duked it out themselves, with the spoils going to whichever half of Vietnam held the Ace of Hearts.

"After a while when you're older you think about how we lost all those lives," Lee muses, and continues.

If you look up the word *Empire* in the dictionary, that's the United States, he explains. We don't want to *own* everything; we just want to *control* everything. Other countries have nuclear power plants, for example, and we check to see if they're using the plants to make bombs. We want to be sure *they* don't have nuclear weapons but *we* do.

Back in the states, service to a country could be better found in ways other than setting oneself up as a target of gunfire. However, Lee believes a voluntary sacrifice of time or talents is vital to a country's well-being.

"I think everyone should serve his country somehow—if not as a soldier, then as a medic or a teacher. Or in the states as a leader of some useful organization—at church or city council."

"Everyone should do something in this country besides mooch off of it," he says.

He gets a little irritated with those who haven't served in any capacity, who refuse to take any type of leadership role, but feel it's their right—regardless of their nonparticipation—to complain about everything.

Lee and others like him have fought for and earned the right to have an opinion about the country and how it's run. Their Purple

Hearts prove it. Years after the fact, their voices—individually or en masse—narrate the wisdom of their collective experience. An experience destined to be repeated in each battle the United States goes to fight—until someone in command hears their battle cry.

But even so... in the end... many of them would do it all again.

Incredibly, this motivation to contribute, to be of service, to make a difference to the world, drives Lee and men and women like him. So much so that if Lee were asked to put on a military uniform once more, he would do so without hesitation.

Lee's feeling of patriotism and love for his country supersedes all that he's been through. The shrapnel embedded in his body coupled with the effects of Agent Orange, and topped off with the terror, isolation, depression, sleeplessness and survivor's guilt of Vietnam, relived through posttraumatic stress disorder and the other multitude of ways Vietnam has disrupted his life.

Lee Heckman stands strong beside the men and women who have picked up weapons in all other wars when asked to fight, in spite of misgivings or fear, just as he will support those who take up weapons to fight the battles of the future.

You can hear his voice now: "Lee Heckman, reporting for duty."

Lee Heckman Awards
(Partial Listing)

Purple Heart

Air Medal

Army Commendation Medal and Letter V Device

Good Conduct Medal

National Defense Service Medal

Vietnam Service Medal

Republic of Vietnam Campaign Ribbon with Device (1960)

Expert Badge and Rifle Bar

If you would like to make a connection with Lee Heckman, you may contact him at (402) 841-6233

About the Author

LaRayne M. Topp is a lifelong resident of Nebraska,
proud of the men and women who have placed their lives on the line
to serve in the United States military,
as well as those who have contributed to the well-being of others
in beneficial ways.

Enjoying the recording of history,
her other books include the following:

*Women at the Reins: Farm Memories based on the Collection
From Mules to Microwaves*
by Cedar Knoll Press

Images of America, Cuming County
by Arcadia Publishing